When the Reaper Calls

A comedy thriller

Peter Colley

Samuel French — London
www.samuelfrench-london.co.uk

ISBN 978-0-573-11477-9

www.samuelfrench.co.uk
www.samuelfrench.com

For Amateur Production Enquiries

United Kingdom and World
excluding North America
plays@samuelfrench.co.uk
020 7255 4302/01

Each title is subject to availability from Samuel French, depending upon country of performance.

WHEN THE REAPER CALLS

First presented at the Gryphon Theatre in Barrie, Ontario, Canada, with the following cast:

Colleen Brandstater	Marguerite Pigott
Professor Victor Pierce	James Carroll
Dora Pierce	Carol Coltman
Professor Harlan Brandstater	Marvin Karon
Officer McGuire	Michael McKeever

Directed by James Douglas
Set designed by Irena and Adam Kolodziej
Costumes designed by Jill Thompson
Lighting designed by James Milburn
Fights directed by John Stead
Sound designed by Laird Fenwick

A revised version was presented at the Upper Canada Playhouse in Morrisburg, Ontario, Canada, with the following cast:

Colleen Brandstater	Stephanie Knight Thomas
Professor Victor Pierce	Stanley Katz
Dora Pierce	Catherine O'Brien
Professor Harlan Brandstater	K. Scott Malcolm
Officer McGuire	Jennifer Fawcett

Directed by Gregson Winkfield
Set designed by Chris Brown and Maggi Macaulay
Costumes designed by Ann Miller
Lighting designed by Rosanne Hicks
Sound designed by Daniel Herridge

CHARACTERS

Professor Victor Pierce, late 20s to early 40s
Dora Pierce, his wife; the same age as Victor
Professor Harlan Brandstater, the same age as Victor
Colleen Brandstater, his wife, early 20s
Officer McGuire, female police officer, early 20s

The action of the play takes place in an old hunting lodge converted to a summer cottage, on the coast of British Columbia, Canada.

SYNOPSIS OF SCENES

ACT I

SCENE 1 Early afternoon on a Friday in summer
SCENE 2 Late evening, the same day

ACT II

That night

Time — the present

"There are only two topics that can be of the least interest to the serious and studious mind — sex and death."

W. B. Yeats

Also by Peter Colley,
published by Samuel French

I'll Be Back Before Midnight

AUTHOR'S NOTE

The initial idea for the play was prompted by the turn of the Millennium — such a notable milestone in the passage of time naturally provokes a long look back at our primitive past, and speculation about our uncertain future.

The two madcap academics in this play have wildly divergent opinions about the future, and especially about the likelihood of life beyond the grave. I wanted their arguments to be a reflection of the hopes and fears we all grapple with, but I have attempted to present their dilemmas in the hopefully entertaining form of a comic mystery.

I also wanted the characters to be a reflection of their past — to show how little the human condition has really changed in the last few thousand years. Despite their high-falutin' chatter, the professors' emotions are still locked into their caveman roots, just as capable of fear, rage, lust, jealousy and revenge as their barbarian ancestors, and quite ready to club each other to death given enough provocation. There's no doubt that mankind has come a long way as architects, builders and scientists — but a quick look at any daily newspaper will reveal that our hearts still live in the dark and dangerous caves of our past.

Peter Colley

For media reviews, playwright's biography and photo
for theatre programmes go to:

www.petercolley.com

A full-colour version of the poster on the cover of this playscript is available free of charge to theatre companies producing this play. The graphics file can be downloaded from the website above.

Artist: Ariel Padilla
Copyright: Peter Colley

ACT I

Scene 1

The living-room of a rough hunting lodge on a remote inlet on the wild and rugged coastline of British Columbia, Canada. Summer. Early afternoon

The lodge has been constructed out of the ruins of an ancient Indian "house", of the type built by the Haida and Nootka of the Pacific Northwest, so the frame is made of irregular logs, and the walls of weathered planking. The lodge was thrown crudely together many years ago as a hunter's shelter and has been converted to a very spartan summer cottage. A primitive kitchen and bathroom have been added (both off stage), but apart from that little has changed. The wind still whistles through the place like the old dried bones of a whale

US, *if possible, a cyclorama should show the changing moods of the sky. Clouds, sunsets, storms and stars can be dramatically evident through the living-room window. Alternatively, a painted backdrop can show the inlet as it winds out to sea, surrounded by distant tree-covered hills*

The living-room is dominated by its large window which overlooks the water, but it has no glass, only an insect screen (the window would be shuttered during bad weather). Large rough-hewn double doors lead out on to a deck. The deck continues under the window, and through the window can be seen the backs of some wooden deckchairs, facing out towards the inlet. Some shrubs are visible through the window and door. A path leads to the deck through the shrubs. The door to a bedroom (Harlan's and Colleen's) is visible R, *and also* R *is a hallway which leads to the offstage kitchen.* L *is a door which leads to Victor's and Dora's bedroom. In the room are a beaten-up sofa and coffee table.* DR *is a small table made out of a tree stump or a wooden crate on which a half-finished chess game is set up, with an easy chair and a wooden crate for the chess players to sit on.* DL *is a crude bar with some bottles, glasses, an old telephone, newspapers, bar stools, and a wastebasket; a list of telephone numbers is pinned up nearby. A light hangs down over the bar. Also in the room are a pile of firewood and a large woodchopper's axe, some more books still in half-unpacked cardboard boxes, and some suitcases which have also not been unpacked; also, a fly-swatter and, by the door, umbrellas*

The walls are adorned with primitive Indian artefacts including a bow with arrows, an Aleutian Indian harpoon, a wall map of the coastline, and a large mercury thermometer on a wooden backing and shelves made from old wooden crates displaying stacks of academic books. A collection of freshly picked herbs stick out of jam jars (used as vases) on a shelf along with some diffusing pots for making herbal tea, etc.

Before the play begins, music plays; this should evoke the songs of the Pacific Northwest Indians and enhance the mood of the cottage as remote and foreboding

When the play begins, summer sunlight pours into the room. The pre-show music fades to be replaced by the sound of gentle wavelets. The cry of a loon echoes across the bay

Professor Victor Pierce enters US *and can be seen through the window coming across the deck towards the double doors. He can be between his late twenties and early forties in age, quite handsome and stylishly dressed in the latest backwoods fashions, including a multi-pocketed fisherman's vest/ waistcoat. Victor is a lovable rogue. He has the kind of delivery that makes it very hard to tell when he's joking, and he carries off his various escapades with great conviction. His nature is basically playful and mischievous, except when interrupted by brief flashes of sadness. He is carrying a fishing tackle box. He looks back to see if anyone is behind him, and then furtively comes into the room through the double doors. He opens the box and takes from it a large silver-coloured pistol (a revolver). He checks the chamber and spins it to make sure it's in working order. He chuckles to himself*

Colleen Brandstater enters through the double doors. She is a very pretty woman in her early twenties, tussle-haired and a little sunburned after a day outside. She is dressed in a casual summer outfit of shorts and T-shirt and carries an old partially-painted wooden Indian mask and a box of paints. She has an endearing innocence about her. Since she never tells lies herself, she assumes that nobody else does either — a dangerous assumption in the company she's presently keeping

Colleen takes Victor by surprise

Colleen Hello, Victor!

Victor jams the pistol back in the tackle box, but he's too late

(*Seeing the gun*) Good heavens!
Victor Oh, hi, Colleen!
Colleen Was that — what I thought it was?
Victor Ah — what did you think it was?
Colleen A gun.

Victor A gun?
Colleen Yes! The thing you just put in the box! It looked like — well — a gun!
Victor Oh, *that*! Why, yes. Now that you ask. It is a gun. A point 44 Magnum.
Colleen Oh! (*Beat*) Are you worried about bears?
Victor Bears! No, no ... The gun is for Harlan.
Colleen Harlan?
Victor Yes. You see, he's going to shoot me tonight.
Colleen I beg your pardon?
Victor Harlan — your darling husband — is going to murder me tonight. That's what the gun's for. Promise me you won't tell him — it's sort of a surprise.
Colleen Harlan is going to murder you ... ?
Victor Yes. A crime of passion. It's quite tragic really. (*He sees something through the window*) Damn it! He's doing it again! (*Shouting out of the window*) Don't you dare touch that fish! (*He runs through the double doors and sprints across the deck*) Put that fish back into the net, Harlan!

Victor exits

Colleen is left looking very bewildered

Dora Pierce enters from the hallway. Dora is an austere woman the same age as Victor. She is dressed in dour, "sensible" clothes of drab tweeds and browns. She was once an attractive woman, but several years of unrelieved surliness have prematurely aged her. Her mood is a simmering, barely-controlled anger — mainly directed against Victor. She is carrying a doctor's bag and some big medical books

The sounds of an argument between Victor and Harlan can be heard from off stage

Victor (*off*) Put it back! I'm warning you, Harlan!

There is an incomprehensible reply from Harlan, off

I intend to eat it, whether it has a soul or not!

The sound of a struggle comes from off stage

Dora (*giving a weary look in the direction of the sound*) What is it this time?
Colleen (*still thinking about Victor; distractedly*) What? I'm sorry ... (*She looks out of the window*) Oh, it's that fish Victor caught. I think Harlan's letting it go.

Dora (*wearily*) Oh no. I can see that this is going to end up as a major debate on the metaphysics of trout. (*She puts down her doctor's bag and places the medical books on a shelf*)

The offstage scuffle heats up

Victor (*off*) I was saving it for my supper, Harlan! Don't ... don't ...

There is the sound of a splash off stage

Oh, damn you!

Dora Amazing, isn't it? They come up here to escape the pressures of university life, and spend most of their time trying to throttle each other.

Professor Harlan Brandstater enters US *and is visible through the window coming across the deck towards the double doors. He is a staid-looking man the same age as Victor, not unattractive, but terminally bland. He wears bifocal glasses, oversize khaki shorts, a dull knit shirt, black shoes, black socks, and a strip of white sunscreen on his nose. He is a soft-spoken academic who studiously avoids displays of violent emotion. Victor follows close behind, splattered with water*

Victor What about yogurt? I've seen you eating that! That's an organism, isn't it? Does that have a soul? Can you hear it scream as it goes down your throat?

Harlan and Victor come into the room through the double doors

Harlan That's not the same, Victor. That's a primitive organism!

Victor Oh, yeah? Well, that fish didn't look so smart to me! (*He sees Dora*) Hello, sweetheart! Did you get some studying done? (*He moves to give Dora a kiss on the cheek*)

Dora Don't come near me! You're soaking! I'll get you a towel.

Dora exits down the hallway

Victor seems a bit hurt by the rebuff at first. Colleen looks at him questioningly, still confused about his talk of murder. Victor sees Colleen looking at him and quickly returns to his usual self, winking at her mischievously

Colleen (*flustered*) Herbal tea, anyone? (*She goes to her jars of herbs and picks some*) I just collected some wild fireweed this morning.

Silence

Harlan?

Harlan (*evasively*) What was that, dear?
Colleen (*waving a soggy sprig at him*) Some wild fireweed tea? It's your favourite.
Harlan (*clearly hating the stuff*) Ah ... fireweed ...
Victor (*bailing him out*) How about some coffee, Colleen? I could really use a cup.
Harlan Yes — a cup of coffee. That would be nice.
Colleen (*realizing she's fighting a losing battle*) OK. I'll make some coffee! But fireweed's a lot healthier.

Colleen waits, but there are no converts. She reluctantly exits to the kitchen

Harlan (*to Victor*) Thanks. I think those herbal teas are rotting my intestines. (*He sits at the unfinished game of chess and stares at the pieces*)
Victor I don't know why I help you at all — the louse who threw away my trout! It was a perfect pan size.
Harlan Don't you think it was cruel keeping it in that net?
Victor Cruel! It's a fish!
Harlan Well, I just couldn't watch it swimming around that little condemned cell, ready to be bludgeoned to death to satisfy your brutish instincts.

Dora enters with a towel

Victor Harlan, hunger is not a brutish instinct. We can't even come up to the cottage without being followed around by your idiotic theories! I hope, when you are reincarnated, that you come back as a trout, and I come back as a bear, and I shall eat you without an ounce of remorse!
Harlan Aha! So you admit to the possibility of reincarnation!
Victor No, I don't!
Harlan You just said it!
Victor I said "if"... "If"! (*To Dora*) Didn't I say "if"?
Dora No.

Dora throws the towel at Victor and heads towards the hallway

Victor (*to Harlan*) Isn't wifely support a wonderful thing?

Victor playfully flicks the towel at Dora as she leaves, but she turns and catches him in the act

Dora If you were reincarnated, Victor, you'd come back as a rat.

Dora exits through the hallway

Victor Well, at least I'm moving up the food chain! Last week I was a cockroach. (*He reacts to seeing a mosquito flying around and picks up the fly swatter*) Harlan, your philosophy is pure superstition.

Harlan Today's superstitions are tomorrow's science.

Victor There's nothing scientific about thinking a fish has a soul! (*He stalks the mosquito during the following*)

Harlan It's never been proved that they don't have one.

Victor I suppose they all have little fish churches down at the bottom of the ocean. Minister Mackerel and the Church Of The Holy Bottom-Feeders. (*In a parson's voice*) "And today's sermon is called: 'Turning The Other Gill'."

Harlan Go on, mock away ...

Victor OK, Harlan, what if it was a thirty-foot shark coming at you? Would you kill it then?

Harlan No. As a Stoic, I'd take my chances.

Victor What about a thirty-foot shark about to attack your lovely young wife? (*He swats at the mosquito and misses, then searches for it again*)

Harlan Victor, a principle's a principle.

Victor You're wrong, Harlan! Everyone is capable of killing in the right circumstances! And not just in self-defence, either.

Harlan If you believe in a soul — as some of us still do — you can't kill anyone. If you believe that there's a time and place where your actions are judged — how can you possibly kill any creature? (*He instinctively slaps his cheek as if squashing the mosquito that has bitten him*)

Victor does not see Harlan killing the mosquito. When Harlan realizes what he's done, he guiltily smears the carcass under the chair arm

Victor There's one thing missing in your argument, Harlan. Passion! In a moment of passion our natural instincts take over and we can do anything — no matter how horrible! All of us are capable of murder! All of us!

Harlan I don't believe that. As Zeno of Citium once said ——

Victor Forget about Zeno — don't you have anything more modern? What about Wittgenstein?

Harlan What about Wittgenstein?

Victor A little case of a red-hot poker.

Harlan Oh, you're not going to bring that up?

Victor Why not? The leading ethics philosopher of the day attacks a rival professor at Cambridge with a red-hot poker. And where did this violent assault take place? The Moral Sciences Club! Proves my point perfectly.

Harlan Wittgenstein didn't attack him. He waved the poker in his general direction. Some say it was more of a toasting fork.

Victor Ah, suddenly you've become a relativist!

Harlan Not at all. Poker or toasting fork — the blow was never actually delivered, which proves my point.

Victor The only reason the blow was never delivered was because there wasn't a woman involved. Do you remember why Wittgenstein went after him?

Harlan Some disagreement over logical positivism, wasn't it?

Victor Logical positivism! Now there's a subject to make your blood boil! But if there had been a woman involved — say, if that professor had been having an affair with Wittgenstein's wife instead of merely disagreeing with his prissy ethics — that poker would not have stopped short — it would have taken his head right off! You see, Harlan, the problem with your pal Zeno was that he didn't have any sex drive. In the real world, all you need is a little intrigue — lust — betrayal — and we could all be trying to hack each other to death before this weekend's out.

Harlan Really, Victor ...

Victor What about tenure? I bet you'd murder me for that!

Harlan (*with a smile*) Ah!

Victor Ah, indeed! That piqued your interest, didn't it? After all, I'm just ahead of you in seniority. Bump me off and you'd get that financial security you crave so much.

Harlan (*laughing*) Don't put ideas into my head!

Victor If you knew you could get away with it, you'd do it!

Dora enters with a tray of muffins and heads towards Harlan

Dora I picked up some fresh muffins in the village. Would you like one, Harlan? (*She heads past Victor to Harlan*)

Victor (*stealing a muffin off the tray*) Thanks! So thoughtful of you! (*To Harlan*) Harlan, we all have something we'd kill for.

Victor exits into his bedroom L, *taking off his wet shirt*

Dora (*watching Victor leave*) Isn't that the truth. (*She offers Harlan the tray of muffins*)

Harlan takes a muffin

Don't expect your coffee any time soon. Colleen's still trying to find that old manual coffee grinder.

Harlan What's wrong with the electric one?

Dora (*imitating Colleen's voice*) "Do you know how many beautiful valleys have been flooded to make the electricity we use?" I'm quoting, of course.

Harlan She has a point.

Dora Your wife is saving the world one cup at a time, while I'm having a hard time even saving myself. (*She picks up her handbag and looks in it, casually at first, and then frantically*) Oh, no!

Harlan What's the matter?

Dora My pills! I left my damn pills at home! God ... I remember now — they were on the sideboard ... ! (*She runs to the telephone and looks at a list of numbers pinned to the wall*) Pharmacy ... Pharmacy ...

Harlan Are you going to be all right?

Dora No! They're my tranquillizers! I go crazy without them! (*She finds the number on the list and dials*) Hello ... I need a prescription filled! … What do you mean — Monday? What kind of pharmacy is that? ..."Joe's Bait, Food and Ammo"? Well, where's the closest one? … Oh, God! … No, it's not an emergency — not yet. … (*She slams the phone down*) A travelling pharmacist — won't be in until Monday! Now I know why they call this the wilderness.

Harlan Will you be OK?

Dora Yes. No. I don't know.

Harlan I didn't know you needed tranquillizers.

Dora Need them? I can't get through a day without them — thanks to my slimeball husband.

Harlan I'd noticed a little tension between you and Victor. We all have.

Dora Little tension? Try murderous rage.

Harlan But why?

Dora Why do you think? He's having another affair.

Harlan Not again! Who is it this time?

Dora I don't know! Does it matter? Some dippy little first year student, no doubt. I've had it with this constant humiliation, Harlan! There are times when I just want to wring his neck!

Harlan Are you sure that he's —— ?

Dora I can tell. For one thing he starts being nice to me. He kisses me on the cheek a lot — calls me "sweetheart" all the time. I've seen these signs before. He's trying to figure out if I'm on to him.

Harlan Oh, dear, oh dear! (*He sits by Dora and reassuringly takes her hand*)

Dora Men! Why can't they all be like you, Harlan? Solid and predictable!

Harlan Well, you have to work at it.

Dora Why did I end up with a wild Epicurean philosophy professor, instead of a nice gentle Stoic like you?

Harlan I don't know what caused Victor to get involved with that way of thinking. One day he was a normal, rational human being — the next he waltzes in and starts rambling on how "Nietzsche was right — God is dead — it's every man for himself!" I thought he was joking — that it was just another one of his games.

Dora It wasn't. We had a good marriage ... He was kind — attentive — loving — and then "bang"!

Harlan You must have talked to him about it?

Dora I've tried — but it's impossible! He can talk forever about philosophy, but he's completely tongue-tied about his own problems.

Harlan It's all so odd. Plato said that when a man is young he obsessively pursues physical beauty, flitting from one passionate chase to another. Then he comes to realize that physical beauty is commonplace and begins his search for goodness and permanence. But Victor seems to be doing it all backwards.

Dora Perhaps I'm not good? I don't feel good. In fact I'm feeling downright wicked these days.

Harlan Oh, you are good, Dora. Take it from an old friend.

Dora Well, to hell with Plato! I can't go on like this, Harlan! I won't just stand by and watch while he parades another affair in front of me! I get so angry sometimes that I don't feel rational anymore. And now I don't have my tranks — we're in for a wild weekend!

Harlan Why don't you talk to Colleen? She makes a herbal tea that's supposed to be a tranquillizer.

Dora You're not serious?

Harlan It would make her feel better if somebody drank the stuff.

Dora I notice you don't.

Harlan I'm not tense.

Dora Not yet, but the night is young. I'm sorry, Harlan. I wish I was more open-minded about that herbal stuff, but I'm not.

Harlan Suit yourself. It's your nerves, not mine. These books of hers claim that it's very efficacious.

Dora It's all a load of bull, Harlan — not an ounce of science in any of it! It's time I proved it to Colleen before she poisons herself and the rest of us. (*She takes one of Colleen's books from a shelf*) Look at these snake-oil books: "Medicines of the Forest — The Shamanic Way to Self-Mastery". (*She looks at another title*) "Spiritwalker — The Herbal Path to Enlightenment". Ha! Can you believe this nonsense? (*She puts the books in her medical bag*) A little creative fiction will be a nice break from my studies.

Harlan Don't be too hard on Colleen, she really believes in all this. Take a few deep breaths — perhaps a walk by the shore? You've been studying awfully hard recently.

Dora (*taking a couple of her medical books from the shelf where she put them earlier and tucking them under her arm*) You needn't worry — I'm the only person in medical school who actually enjoys the workload. It distracts me from my overwhelming desire to strangle my husband.

Dora picks up her doctor's bag and exits through the double doors

Harlan sits at the chessboard again

Victor pops his head around his bedroom door

Victor Has she gone?
Harlan Yes. She's studying down at the boathouse.

Victor comes into the room. He has changed into a dry shirt

Victor What did she say?
Harlan Now, Victor! You know I can't tell you what she told me in confidence.
Victor No need to, old chum! She thinks I'm having an affair. (*He sits at the chessboard and stares at the pieces*)
Harlan Are you?
Victor No! Nothing could be further from the truth! I'm *trying* to have an affair, and failing miserably!
Harlan Victor, Victor! Why do you do this?
Victor Pretty obvious, isn't it? Dora's hardly been a barrel of laughs recently. I think that scowl is becoming a permanent fixture.
Harlan Don't forget, you were the one who changed, Victor!
Victor Me? I haven't changed! (*He starts to move a chess piece, but then changes his mind and stops*)
Harlan Don't you remember? The day you decided that between Epicurus and Nietzsche you had all the answers.
Victor Oh, that. I've just come to my senses, that's all. But when it comes to the "change" department, you are the Dean of the Faculty.
Harlan What do you mean?
Victor You've completely lost your sense of fun. You never play pranks any more. (*During the following he goes to the bar and gets himself a drink, then pours one for Harlan*)
Harlan We're too old for that sort of thing. Besides, your pranks have become very dark and strange in recent years. It's that dreadful nihilism of yours.
Victor You call it nihilism — I call it realism.
Harlan How can you be so certain that there's nothing out there?
Victor Harlan, I may not know everything, but I sure know nothing when I see it. We've all been tricked; there's nothing out there but a house of dust — a worm's pasture! (*He crosses to Harlan, gives him the drink, and sits by the chessboard*)
Harlan I don't understand what's happened to you! You used to be an open-minded idealist — you were also never the type to be unfaithful to his wife, and then suddenly you went out and had that affair with that Hanley girl.

Victor Oh, I started it all, did I? As always, I'm the villain. But that's not the whole story, Harlan.
Harlan Then what is the whole story?

Victor makes to say something, then stops. There is a pause

Victor Forget about it, Harlan! Let's just say we're all slaves to our baser instincts.
Harlan We're not slaves … We have choices ... You have choices ...
Victor I don't think so. Ah, who cares? We're simply a true reflection of life — chaotic, irrational, murderous and completely beyond hope.
Harlan Murderous?
Victor Did I say murderous? Well, I'm sure it fits in there somewhere. In a way all this has been a liberation. Now I see life as it really is. We're all animals — racing around in an orgy of self-gratification until we drop dead from excess or boredom. And now my greatest challenge is to prove that simple fact to you.
Harlan And my greatest challenge is to prove to you that you're wrong. In fact, I have a quote from Kierkegaard that even you would find appropriate. (*He heads towards his bedroom*)
Victor Kierkegaard! I didn't think you read any books that were less than two thousand years old.
Harlan (*stopping*) I like to know what I'm up against.
Victor You're so certain, aren't you? That's why you're such an antique. Modern philosophy begins with doubt.
Harlan I know: "Doubt everything that can be doubted". Descartes makes an interesting point, but I happen to believe it all begins with faith. Then doubt if faith fails.
Victor When faith fails.
Harlan Let me get that quote.
Victor You won't find the answer in any of those books! Only in life.

Harlan exits into his bedroom

Victor gets up and looks around to make sure he's alone. He takes the pistol out of the tackle box, twirls it like a cowboy, sticks it in his pocket, and does a "quick draw"

Pow, pow, pow! (*He looks at the pistol*) All tragedies are ended by a death — all comedies by a marriage! (*He puts the gun to his head*) Bang!

Colleen enters through the hallway, proudly juggling a tray with several cups of coffee on it

Colleen I made the coffee! I even added some fresh-picked chicory. (*She looks around at the empty room*) Oh!

Victor puts the pistol on the chess table

Victor They're both busy, as usual. It's just you and me.

Colleen (*putting the coffee tray down*) Now, Victor, what on earth were you talking about? Murder? Harlan shooting you? What are you up to now?

Victor Oh that! I'm sorry I had to spring it on you like that, but I was going to tell you anyway. It's a little experiment of mine. It's perfectly safe — I'm putting blanks in the gun, of course. But it's time Harlan stopped deluding himself and saw the truth.

Colleen Victor, I can't simply stand by and watch you pull some cruel trick on him!

Victor It's not cruel! He enjoys a game as much as anyone! You should have seen the stunts he's pulled on me over the years. He was an extraordinary games player before he turned into a potted plant. (*He picks up the Indian mask that Colleen brought in earlier and looks at it like the skull in "Hamlet"*) "Alas poor Harlan! I knew him, Horatio. He was a fellow of infinite jest." Colleen, there was a time when he was one of the greatest pranksters you ever met. In our university days he was inspired — a genuinely twisted imagination ...

Colleen This is my Harlan you're talking about?

Victor The same. But in recent years he's become just as dead as this character here. (*To the mask, in Shakespearian style*) "Where be your gibes now? Your gambols? Your flashes of merriment that would set the table on a roar?" (*He sighs and tosses the mask aside on the sofa*)

Colleen tries to grab the mask, nervous about its fragility

I miss him, Colleen. And you would too, if you'd known him then. Bit by bit, all the pieces of my life I ever cared about are falling away.

Colleen (*putting the mask in a safe place*) And you think this game will bring Harlan back?

Victor It's our only chance. Shock therapy.

Colleen Our only chance?

Victor Yes! You're in this too. This stoicism is ruining him. He's so obsessed with the next life that he's stopped living this one. Look how he treats you — you're young and beautiful and energetic, and yet he hardly seems to know you exist!

Colleen That's not true!

Victor OK, when was the last time he took you out for a romantic evening? When was the last time he wrote wild poetry for you? When was the last time he even told you he loved you?

Colleen Well ... Umm ... But Stoics don't do things like that.
Victor But Harlan *isn't* a Stoic! That's the whole point! He's as volatile and passionate as I am — more so!
Colleen No, I'm sorry, Victor, I can't go along with this. (*She moves away from Victor and takes a book from a shelf. It's a large book called "Herbs of the Northwest" with colourful plants on its cover. She sits and opens the book*)
Victor You're not going to cure him with one of your herbal concoctions, much as though you try.

Colleen looks at Victor

Oh, yes, I'm on to you, my girl. There's a lot more than fireweed you're putting in that tea. (*Taking the book out of her hand*) Tell me what he usually does when he gets home! Does he rush up to you and kiss you madly?
Colleen (*grabbing the book back*) You know he doesn't!
Victor Sometimes he doesn't even say hello, does he? He just goes straight to his study, and starts working. I've been there — I've seen it.
Colleen (*rapidly flicking through the book*) Sometimes he does that.
Victor Now imagine a Harlan coming home like this. It's the end of the working day. You've been home all day, alone. You've been dabbling with your paints and your masks, trimming your herb garden, doing your yoga, but you're bored — you're lonely. You see Harlan's car pull up outside. (*He dashes outside on to the deck and plays at being Harlan during the following. Speaking through the screen window*) He gets out of the car — rushes up the walkway, tears off his tie (*he mimes this*) — rips off his jacket. He kicks open the door! (*He kicks open the double doors*) Lust is in his eyes — his breathing is heavy — he's sweating. (*He wipes the sweat from his forehead*) As his eyes fix on you, you feel the electricity of an animal in heat! He rushes to your side (*he rushes to Colleen*) — he throws his arms around you. He says things like ——

Dora enters US *and crosses the deck, visible through the screen window. It is plain she can clearly hear the following*

— I love you, Colleen. You are the most beautiful woman I've ever seen.

Dora stops in her tracks and stares at Victor and Colleen in horror through the screen window

I thought of nothing but you all day. I couldn't wait to get here so we could make love the whole night through. From now on we're going to make love under the stars — go skinny-dipping in the ocean. No more books, no more papers — just you and me and a life of unbridled passion! What do you think?

Victor's playacting has aroused feelings in Colleen that she has been suppressing for a long time. Her book slips from her grasp and crashes to the floor. Dora backs away into the foliage beyond the deck

(*Referring to Colleen's far-away expression*) Colleen? Colleen?

Colleen (*distractedly*) Wha... what? I'm sorry...

Victor What do you think? Isn't it better this way? (*He indicates the pistol on the chessboard*)

Colleen (*confused*) Ah ... Yes ... (*She sees the pistol*) No ... God, I don't know ... (*She picks up her book from the floor*)

Dora's face slowly appears in a corner of the window

Victor So you won't tell Harlan that I've put blanks in the gun?

Colleen You're absolutely sure it's safe?

Victor What could go wrong? All I want to do is to prove to Harlan that he's capable of pulling that trigger! I'm the one who's at risk — he'll be aiming the gun at me!

Colleen I don't know...

Victor It'll be good for both of us. He'll see who he really is — you'll see who he really is — and then we can all stop this idiotic pretence, and move on with our lives. You deserve to have some romance back in your life, and if you let me I can give it to you.

Colleen But guns terrify me ... What if ... ? (*She turns away from Victor and moves towards the window*)

Dora quickly backs away into the shadows of the foliage

Victor His stoicism is only going to get worse. This may be our last chance to make a breakthrough. Please don't tell him! Please!

Colleen looks hesitant

(*Taking her hesitancy as a "yes"*) Thank you! (*He kisses Colleen on the cheek, takes the pistol from the chess table and puts it back in the fishing tackle box*)

Colleen Victor ! Now stop that. I haven't said ——

Victor You won't regret it!

Victor bounds excitedly to his bedroom and exits

Colleen tries to pull herself together, then exits through the hallway

After a moment Dora comes in quietly through the double doors

Dora So that's who it is! Colleen! (*Looking towards Victor's bedroom*) The lousy, two-timing weasel! (*She goes over to the fishing tackle box and takes out the pistol*) Blanks, hmm? (*She flips open the pistol's chamber and spins it, with a cold laugh*)

Harlan enters from his bedroom, carrying a philosophy book

Dora quickly hides the pistol behind her back

Harlan Is everything OK?
Dora (*stifling her laugh*) Yes. Fine. (*She bursts into laughter again*)

Harlan looks down to see if his fly is open

It's not you, Harlan. (*She laughs again*) It's just something funny I thought of. (*She laughs wickedly*)

The Lights fade. Ominous music punctuates the end of the scene, continuing through the Black-out

Scene 2

The same. Several hours later that evening

The Lights come up. The bright sunlight of Scene 1 has now changed to the golden glow of the setting sun; during the scene the Lights fade to twilight and then to complete night with moonlight. The interior lights are on, as is the light over the bar. The half-unpacked cardboard boxes and suitcases have been put away. There is now a plastic shopping bag in the wastebasket with the words, "Joe's Bait, Food & Ammo" on it, and, on the deck, a copy of the magazine "Fish Facts Monthly" and a fishing rod

Harlan is fast asleep on the sofa, a large volume of Plato's "Apology" lying open on his stomach. His bifocal glasses are perched on his forehead and his head is thrown back, his mouth wide open as he snores softly

Victor enters US *on to the deck. He peeks into the room through the screen window and sees Harlan. He comes into the room through the double doors, tiptoes over to the fishing tackle box and takes out the pistol. Victor looks at the pistol with a smile, then tiptoes quietly over to Harlan and glances at the book lying on his stomach*

Victor (*reading the title*) Plato's *Apology*. Well, he should apologize — look what he's done to you! (*Whispering into Harlan's ear*) You are going to kill Victor ! He is your enemy — you hate him! You will pick up a silver pistol and shoot him right through his black heart! (*He laughs to himself*) "If you believe in a soul, you can't kill anyone." We'll see about that! (*He looks around for a good place to put the pistol. He places it strategically on the chess table*)

Victor exits into his bedroom L

There comes the sound of a door opening and closing off stage from Harlan and Colleen's bedroom R, *indicating that their room has a door which leads to the outside*

Colleen enters through the bedroom door, carrying her box of paints and the Indian mask she's been working on; it is now fully painted and has a sly grin. Colleen sees Harlan sleeping, then notices the pistol on the chess table and reacts nervously. She coughs to get Harlan's attention. It doesn't work. She goes back to the door and slams it

Harlan wakes up with a sudden snort and starts reading right where he left off

Colleen Harlan?
Harlan Oh, hello! I was just reading. (*He squints at the text and then looks around for his glasses which are perched on his forehead. Finally, he finds them*)
Colleen I have to talk to you, Harlan.
Harlan Certainly.
Colleen There's something you should ... You see, Victor is ... That is, we were ... Ah... (*Losing her nerve*) Do you like my mask? (*She shows him the mask*)
Harlan (*barely glancing at the mask*) Yes, yes. Very nice. (*He puts his nose back into his book*)
Colleen Harlan, you're not listening to me!
Harlan (*looking up*) I'm sorry. What was it you said?
Colleen My mask ...
Harlan Ah, yes. (*He squints at it*) Pretty. Very pretty.
Colleen (*offended*) Pretty!?
Harlan Ah ... Maybe that wasn't quite the right word ... It's — (*looking closely at the mask*) very — dramatic?

Beat. Colleen glares at Harlan

What does it ... Ah — who does it represent?

Colleen It's a trickster spirit — Puk-wudji, I think. (*She puts her box of paints on a shelf and looks around for a place to hang the mask on the wall during the following*)

Harlan (*trying to show interest*) Puk-wudji?

Colleen He's the nephew of Guguyni, the Raven — he loves to play tricks, and tell secrets. He's also a transformer — he can turn himself into anything — so you have to keep an eye on him.

Harlan Where did you get it? It looks quite old.

Colleen It was on the wall of the hardware store in the village — they said it was found right around here. It was in terrible condition, the paint was all worn off.

Harlan Is that wise — painting it, I mean? Aren't those old masks supposed to have spirits? Tinkering with them may be dangerous.

Colleen I did some chants over it to drive away any bad spirits.

Harlan Ah, your yoga chants, yes. Very prudent.

Colleen No, I used a real Indian chant. Remember that shamanism class I took? And I'm using paints I made from native plants — I'm just trying to restore it to its original condition. Besides, you told me this whole cottage was made out of the remains of a sacred Nootka long-house and nobody has ever come to any harm here. (*Beat*) Have they?

Harlan Not that I've heard of. Although I've often wondered why the rent is so much lower than the other cottages.

Colleen What! (*She looks around apprehensively*)

Harlan Still, we've been coming here for years without any problems. Yes, I'm sure we're all perfectly safe and sound.

Colleen Spirits are very patient. They could be waiting for the right moment. I'll look up some chants for houses — just in case.

Harlan Good idea. (*Pleasantly*) Well, back to work. (*He goes back to his book*)

Colleen finds an empty hook on the wall and hangs the mask on it

Colleen Harlan ... Do you think I'm "pretty"?

Harlan Everyone thinks you're pretty, Colleen.

Colleen I'm not interested in what everyone thinks, I want to know what you think!

Harlan Of course I think you're pretty, but I didn't marry you because of something so superficial as beauty.

Colleen I know that, Harlan — I didn't mean to suggest ... (*Beat*) Why did you marry me?

Harlan You know why I married you. There were many, many reasons. Yes, indeed. (*Thinking he's satisfied her, he goes back to his book*)

Colleen How about giving me one!

Harlan Oh, golly — you mean right now?

Colleen It's not a trick question, you know.

Harlan Very well. (*He thinks hard*) When I met you, you were like a ... (*He struggles for the right word*)

Colleen Yes?

Harlan A breath of fresh air. You were — invigorating.

Colleen You make me sound like an aerosol spray.

Harlan I'm not very good at this sort of thing. I need some time to think about it.

Colleen How long? A couple of minutes? I'll wait. (*She sits next to Harlan, waiting*)

Harlan Darling, now isn't a very good time. I'm in the middle of preparing this new course on the Megarian philosophers and their conditional propositions.

Colleen Harlan, please! I wouldn't interrupt your studies if it wasn't important! It's just that — sometimes I'm not sure ... I'm not sure just how much you really love me!

Harlan Now, what put that into your head?

Colleen I have to know that you love me! I have to!

Harlan Ah! Love? Well, that's a complex emotion, metaphysically speaking. That single word is probably the most misused and dangerous utterance in the English language.

Colleen Dangerous! I'm talking about you and me, Harlan, not ... (*Pause*) Not what happened to you in the past.

Harlan (*sensing the inference*) Meaning?

Colleen I'm not Helen.

Harlan No, thank heavens.

Colleen So I'm not dangerous. So you can say "I love you" without putting your entire psyche at risk. Now, I don't want to put words into your mouth, but a wife needs to hear it said once in a while. And *now* would be a very good time. If you felt it, of course. (*Pause*) What I mean is, if you're waiting for a more opportune time to say it — (*with an edge*) *don't*!

Harlan (*squirming under the intensity of her gaze*) You're right. I'm sorry. That whole nonsense with (*finding it difficult to even say her name*) He... Hel... Helen... has made me a little gun-shy about verbalizing my emotions. Love. Yes, I can do this. Why not? (*He gets up, takes a deep breath, then loses his nerve, talking to Colleen as if addressing his students*) Let's start by defining it. Love. Are we using Aristophanes' theory, Socrates' rejoinder or Plato's definition?

Colleen Please, Harlan! Not now!

Harlan But love means so many different things that you can't just use a word as powerful as that without making sure that our terminology is compatible. Even Plato is not as straightforward as people think; for example the French — who do know a little about love — have distinguished between *amour platonique* and *amour platonicien* ——

Colleen Oh, God! (*She gets up and makes to leave*)

Harlan Colleen! Wait! What is it? You seem upset.

Colleen It's nothing. I get strange thoughts sometimes. It's just something Victor and I were talking about.

Harlan (*his eyes narrowing*) Victor?

Colleen Harlan, ever since we've been married, you've been busy preparing one course or another — or writing papers. I've tried to be understanding — I've never made any demands on you, but — will there be a time when you're not busy?

Harlan It's publish or perish in the academic world. I have to do a lot of work.

Colleen So this isn't going to change?

Harlan What isn't going to change, dearest?

Colleen Oh, never mind ...

Colleen struggles to hide her anguish, then turns and exits quickly through the hallway

Harlan (*following her*) Colleen! Colleen!

Harlan exits through the hallway

Dora peers in from the double doors and then comes quietly into the room carrying a handbag. She glances around to make sure she is alone and then goes to the tackle box. Finding the gun gone, she looks around for it. She sees it lying on the chess table and picks it up. She goes over to the bar, flips open the chamber and — her actions just hidden by the top of the bar — removes Victor's blanks and replaces them with something out of her handbag

You are in for a big surprise, my little tom-cat!

Harlan appears outside on the deck, visible through the screen window, looking around desperately. He pokes his head in through the double doors

Hearing the door open, Dora quickly puts the pistol on the bar and stands in front of it

Dora Oh! It's you.

Harlan Did Colleen come through here?

Dora No.

Harlan (*sighing*) Oh, dear, oh, dear! (*He turns to leave*)
Dora What's the matter?

Harlan stops, then comes into the living-room

Harlan I said the wrong thing, as usual.
Dora What was it this time?
Harlan Oh, it's that "love" thing. It's such a complicated word.
Dora Not to a woman, it isn't.
Harlan I was simply trying to define ——
Dora (*losing it*) *Oh, shut up*, Harlan! Forget about your stupid definitions and just tell her you love her. I'm sure that's all she wants. Men! You all drive me crazy! It isn't a big deal! (*She grabs Harlan and shakes him*) She wants you to say something very simple: she wants you to say "I love you, Colleen." That's all! (*She beats him on the chest*) "*I love you*, Colleen!" What's so damn hard about that?
Harlan (*staring at her in shock*) How long has it been since your last tranquillizer?
Dora *Nine o' clock this morning!* (*She calms down and lets go of Harlan*) I'm sorry, Harlan. You're right, I am a bit irrational. But this lack of passion of yours is very dangerous. Dangerous to all of us.
Harlan Dangerous?
Dora Yes. It leaves a very attractive young wife drifting out there in the emotional wilderness, desperate to feel loved, to feel wanted — thirsting for something — anything — to fill the void. Nature abhors a vacuum, Harlan.
Harlan Hmm. I see what you mean.
Dora You've got to get your butt off the sidelines and get back into the game.
Harlan You're right, of course.
Dora So you agree? You'll do it?
Harlan Yes, I'll do it!
Dora Off you go then!

Harlan dutifully trots off down the hallway and exits

(*To herself*) Of course, it may be too late for some of us.

Officer McGuire, a young policewoman, enters US *on the deck; she is visible through the screen window. She looks almost too young to be in the police, and her uniform seems a bit too big for her. She makes up for this by being extremely earnest and devoid of humour — standing very upright and determined to appear as tough as nails. The truth is: she's desperate to make the first arrest of what she expects to be an illustrious law enforcement career. She knocks loudly on the double doors*

Dora wheels around nervously and sees Officer McGuire standing out on the deck. Suddenly panicked, Dora runs back to the bar, grabs the pistol and — her actions hidden by the bar — quickly takes the bullets out of the pistol and puts them back into her handbag. She desperately looks around for a place to hide the pistol

Officer McGuire knocks again, loudly, and with more urgency than before

In a panic Dora puts the pistol on the bar and covers it with a newspaper. She cautiously opens the double doors

Oh, hello! Can I help you?

Officer McGuire I'm Officer McGuire. Are you the owner of this cottage?

Dora No. We rent it. Is there a problem?

Officer McGuire We're warning the cottagers: there's been some thefts in the area — a tricycle and two canoe paddles so far.

Dora (*sarcastically*) Really? I'm surprised I didn't hear about it on the evening news.

Officer McGuire He won't get far, I'll see to that.

Dora Not with two paddles and a tricycle, he won't!

Officer McGuire (*eyeing Dora coldly*) You don't seem to take criminal acts very seriously, madam.

Dora Are you old enough to join the police?

Officer McGuire (*annoyed — she's been asked this before*) I'm old enough to vote, and I'm old enough to fight and kill for my country, if that answers your question!

Dora Yes, it certainly does! (*She glances uneasily towards the pistol*)

Officer McGuire senses the tension in the air which piques her police instincts — as does her instant dislike of Dora

Officer McGuire (*looking around suspiciously*) So — everything all right here?

Dora Yes. Everything's fine. Terrific in fact. Couldn't be better.

Officer McGuire Uh-huh. Where are you people from?

Dora Vancouver. City folk.

Officer McGuire (*slowly moving around, eyes scanning the room*) Are you aware that the brush around the cottage should have been cleared by now?

Dora Really?

Officer McGuire There's a fire alert. The drought, you know.

Dora Ah, the drought.

Officer McGuire When you see the owner, tell him he'll get a citation if it's not cleared by next week.

Dora Yes ... I'll tell him.

Officer McGuire moves to a shelf full of books, glancing at the titles

Officer McGuire Not the usual cottage reading material.
Dora Our husbands are professors at U.B.C.
Officer McGuire (*with a snort of derision*) Eggheads, eh? (*She looks at a book*) Huh. *The Age Of Reason.*
Dora Philosophy.
Officer McGuire Uh-huh. (*Seeing another book*) "Herbs of the Northwest". Philosophy?
Dora Herbs.
Officer McGuire (*wheeling on Dora, accusingly*) What kind of herbs?
Dora For tea. We don't smoke them.
Officer McGuire (*seeing another book*) Gray's *Anatomy*?
Dora Anatomy. I'm in medical school.

Officer McGuire looks blankly at the half-finished game on the chessboard

Chess.
Officer McGuire Thank you. (*She sees the harpoon on the wall; touches the point*) That could do some damage in the wrong hands.
Dora It's a harpoon. Indian, I suppose. It's an antique.

Officer McGuire takes one more sniff around and sees the barrel of the pistol sticking out from under the newspaper on the bar

Officer McGuire Hello! What's this? (*She pushes aside the paper, picks up the pistol and admires it — she obviously loves guns*) A point 44 Magnum, single-action revolver, five-inch barrel, chrome finish, adjustable rear sights. (*She strokes it erotically*) Nice — very nice — (*breaking out of her reverie*) But not an antique.
Dora It's my husband's.
Officer McGuire (*flipping out the gun's chamber — it's empty*) Does he have a licence for this?
Dora Of course. We're Canadian.
Officer McGuire I'd like to take a look at it. This is a restricted firearm, you know. He has to be a member of an approved shooting club ——
Dora — or a registered collector. He's both. Loves his guns.
Officer McGuire Where is he?
Dora God only knows. I'm only his wife. Anyway, it's not loaded. It's really just a toy to him. He never brings ammunition.

Officer McGuire puts the pistol back on the bar. She sees the "Joe's Ammo" plastic bag in the wastebasket. She holds the bag up to show Dora

Officer McGuire No ammunition, eh?
Dora "Joe's *Bait, Food* and Ammo." The worms are on special. If you hurry there may be some left.
Officer McGuire *You* bought worms?
Dora What? Don't I look like the worm type? You'd be surprised. I'm very familiar with worms.
Officer McGuire Like to fish, do you?
Dora No.

Officer McGuire flips out a notebook and scribbles in it

Officer McGuire I'll come back later. Ask him to find that licence, would you? I want to see it. (*She moves to the door*) And don't forget to tell the others not to leave things out at night.
Dora I won't.

Officer McGuire does one more scan around the room, scribbles some more in her notebook, and then goes on to the deck through the double doors. Dora heaves a sigh of relief, closes the double doors, and rushes towards the pistol. Officer McGuire picks up the fishing rod from the deck and, holding it, knocks on the double doors. Dora opens the doors. Officer McGuire hands the rod to Dora with a chiding look —i.e. "Don't leave things out at night" — and then heads off across the deck, turning to glance suspiciously through the screen window. Dora waves at her with a big fake smile

Officer McGuire stomps off down the path and disappears off stage

Dora runs back to the bar, grabs the pistol and stuffs the bullets back into the chamber — again hiding her actions under the edge of the bar counter. She puts the pistol back on the bar

Victor enters from his bedroom

Victor Was that a policeman? (*He looks out of the window*)
Dora Woman. One of our stalwart girls in blue. Very stalwart. I'm surprised you missed her.
Victor Well, I can't catch them all, can I? What did she want?
Dora She says you shouldn't leave your tricycle out at night.
Victor What?
Dora Apparently there's an artful dodger who has the whole coast a-tremble, but gallant Officer McGuire is hot on the trail.

Victor (*nervously glancing at the chessboard where the gun was last placed*) She didn't see my gun, did she?

Dora (*after a beat*) No. I hid it by the bar. You can shoot away to your heart's content.

Victor Good. All I want to do is to bag a few rabbits. You'd think that was the crime of the century the way the cops are these days. (*He sits at the chess table and stares at the pieces*)

Dora Well, be careful where you aim. I'll be out this evening, along with the rabbits.

Victor (*surprised*) Out?

Dora Yes. There's a Women's Guild lecture in the village on "Men Who Are Pigs and The Women Who Love Them". I'd like to catch it.

Victor I'm sure you would, darling. That phenomenon is more common than people realize.

Dora So I'm told. It'll probably go on quite late.

Victor No doubt.

Dora You'll be left to your own devices, I'm afraid.

Victor I'm sure I'll find some mischief to get into.

Dora You're such a trooper. You and Harlan can catch up on some debating while I'm out. You haven't argued for at least an hour.

Victor I have a feeling we're going to settle our grand debate once and for all tonight. (*He moves a piece on the chess board, and smiles*)

Dora I can't wait to get back and see how it turned out. (*She looks at the chessboard*) If you keep that move you could lose your queen. In fact you could lose the whole game.

Victor (*staring at the board*) I can't see that, Dora!

Dora I know. I'll see you later. (*She heads for the double doors*)

Victor Dora?

Dora Yes?

They look at each other for a moment. Victor seems to want to talk, but can't

Victor Oh, nothing. Enjoy yourself! The forecast is for thunderstorms — you'd better take an umbrella.

Dora is momentarily surprised at this brief flash of concern. She takes an umbrella from beside the door, and then exits

Victor stares at the chessboard to see what Dora meant — but can't. He goes over to the bar and picks up the pistol and carefully places it on the chessboard

By now the evening light has darkened into twilight — soon it will be completely dark

Dora and Harlan can be heard talking outside some distance away, off stage. They enter US, *approaching the cottage along the path*

Victor hears the voices and sees Dora and Harlan through the screen window. He goes to the window to eavesdrop

Dora exits

Harlan nears the cottage, coming on to the deck. Victor scoots back into the centre of the room. Harlan opens the double doors and comes into the room

Victor Talking to Dora, were you? About me, I'll bet.
Harlan No, we were talking about Colleen.
Victor Colleen? Having problems, are you?
Harlan (*defensively*) No.
Victor You're such a liar! What a sanctimonious old fart you've become.
Harlan Victor !
Victor Harlan, has it ever crossed your mind that I've never really liked you?
Harlan No. Of course not.
Victor Well, I suppose never "liked" isn't quite the right word. It would be more accurate to say I despise you — is that any clearer?

Harlan looks at Victor closely: is he joking?

During the following, Victor manipulates Harlan so that he is right by the chessboard where the pistol is lying

Harlan Look, I'm sorry I had to let your fish go ...
Victor This has nothing to do with that! I've never liked you. Fish or no fish!
Harlan I know you're having a hard time with Dora ...
Victor It has nothing to do with Dora, either! It has a lot to do with you.
Harlan (*seeing the gun on the chessboard; shocked*) Is that a gun?
Victor Yes. I thought I'd make a rabbit stew for the carnivores among us. And don't give me any crap about small furry ghosts following me to my grave.
Harlan It's not small furry ghosts you have to worry about—it's the police. You really shouldn't bring your handguns up here. You know I don't like them, and hunting anything with them is illegal.
Victor To hell with the cops! Besides, who's going to find out? Unless you're thinking of squealing on me.
Harlan Victor, what's the problem? Have I done something to upset you?
Victor What has happened to me, Harlan, is more in the nature of a revelation. A revelation that you are that most despicable of philosophers — a hypocrite.

Harlan is taken aback for a moment

Harlan Ahh ... You're not going to get to me, Victor! I know your little games.

Victor This is no game! For the first time, I see you as you really are. You're a fraud! Everyone else saw it but me! For years I defended you within the faculty. I defended you when I saw your students laughing behind your back! I suppose you didn't realize that?

Harlan I know you've stood by me, and I appreciate that. I'm well aware that I have my detractors. I'm old-fashioned, I suppose. I don't teach a popular course like you do. But I do try to teach them the truth.

Victor So it doesn't bother you that you're a laughing stock?

Harlan What can I do?

Victor (*mocking*) "What can I do?" "What can I do?" Is that all you can say? You know you're a fraud, don't you? That's why you never fight for what you believe in! That's why you never stand up for yourself! You think you can shrug it off by claiming to be a Stoic. Christ, no wonder Helen left you!

Harlan (*shocked*) Victor !

Victor What? Oh, right ... You don't like me to mention your "ex".

Harlan I don't see what she has to do with all this.

Victor She has a lot to do with it. Thesis: your whole philosophy is based upon your hiding from the truth!

Harlan You know perfectly well, I've devoted my life to searching for the truth. We both have.

Victor The truth? OK, let's examine that. You claim that you believe in non-violence. Then let me remind you of a little incident that you may have forgotten. About three years ago ... May twenty-third, I think the date was. You know what I'm talking about, don't you? Or have you — in your new relativist universe — conveniently forgotten?

Harlan I haven't forgotten.

Victor Very unpleasant thing to witness! A professor attacking a student like that.

Harlan It wasn't an attack ... I never meant to hurt that boy.

Victor No — you meant to kill him! And do you remember why you attacked that student?

Harlan I told you, I didn't attack him ... He'd been insolent, that's all ...There were words — some shoving went on ...!

Victor You're just like Wittgenstein ... (*Imitating Harlan*) "Oh, no, it wasn't a red-hot poker, it was a toasting fork". Let me tell you about your "shoving"! I nearly had to break your fingers to get your hand off his throat! You were trying to shove him into his grave!

Harlan No! It wasn't like that!

Victor But what was the boy being insolent about, Harlan? What was the subject of his insolence?

Harlan Stop it, Victor! (*Trying to turn away from Victor, he sits by the chessboard*)

Victor looms behind Harlan — now he has him exactly where he wants him with the pistol right in front of him

Victor Perhaps I should jog your memory! It was the day after Helen left you. She'd run off with that fellow on the football team. Or was it volleyball? Anyway, the boy you attacked had set you off by mentioning it. (*He moves in front of Harlan — a perfect target*) What was that boy's name? Tomlins, wasn't it? I can just hear him now: (*putting on a nasal voice*) "Professor Brandstater, we haven't seen as much of your charming wife as we're used to. Has she been taken sick or something? Me and the other guys in the dorm were wondering: does this mean she's not going to tuck us in every night like she used to? We're really going to miss that!"

Harlan That's a damned lie! He never said that!

Victor You see that boy knew — like we all knew — that your darling Helen would have jumped on anything with a heartbeat — because she was, in a word, a slu ...

Harlan Don't say it, Victor ... !

Victor And now you're too terrified to commit to Colleen, or even to any philosophy that actually includes "living" — and you've even frozen *me* out of your goddamned life — and all because Helen was a slut ...!

Harlan Shut up! *Shut up!*

Harlan, in a surge of violent passion, grabs the pistol from the chess table, scattering chess pieces everywhere, and aims the pistol right at Victor's heart. There is a tense moment in which it seems Harlan is going to shoot, but then he abruptly regains control

Do you really think that about Colleen and me?

Victor Yes.

Harlan Then we're well matched. You're only a hedonist out of some misguided rage against Dora.

Victor That's not true!

Harlan I could have shot you, you know. The only thing that stopped me was my awareness of my own anger. I'm a Stoic. If I ever do shoot you, it'll be rationally.

Harlan puts the pistol back on the chess table, and exits through the hallway

Victor Damn! (*He paces angrily*) Damn!

Colleen enters through the double doors

Colleen I have to talk to you, Victor! You must stop this!
Victor Have you been eavesdropping?
Colleen No, I was outside picking herbs, but I could hear Harlan shouting. You have to stop goading him! It's just not fair to him!

Victor considers for a moment

Victor You're right. I've gone too far. I'm sorry.
Colleen He didn't try to shoot you, did he? You see! I knew he wasn't that kind of person.
Victor Perhaps I misjudged him. Just like Wittgenstein and his poker, he stopped short.
Colleen Who?
Victor Oh, nothing. (*Beat*) Damn!
Colleen So it's over?
Victor (*with distaste*) Over! (*Beat. He hates to lose*) Yes, I suppose so. (*Thinking hard, he picks up one of the fallen chess pieces*)
Colleen You're taking it so well. It takes a big man to admit he's wrong.
Victor (*it's killing him*) Yes. I have no problem admitting I'm wrong. *(The tension he feels from saying the last word causes him to break the chess piece gripped in his hand into two with a sharp snap. He tries to jam the broken pieces together. Failing, he puts the two broken parts back on one square of the chessboard. Trying to think of a way out*) So ... Maybe Harlan really is over this Helen thing.
Colleen What? What Helen thing?
Victor Oh, you know — this inability to love. I guess he's over it now. (*Slyly*) No need to try and change him.
Colleen I've never met this Helen, but I feel like I'm sharing a house with her.
Victor You are. A one-woman wrecking crew if ever there was one. Mind you, Harlan brought it on himself. Neglected her needs. Neglect can turn even good people into monsters.
Colleen That's no excuse for what she did to him. She should have just divorced him rather than running around the way she did. Of course he was hurt and jealous — who wouldn't be?
Victor He was jealous all right. Boy was he jealous! (*Looking at Colleen and having an idea*) Listen, Colleen — you want me to stop the game? Is that what you truly want?
Colleen Oh, I don't know what I want! I don't want you to hurt him, and yet — if I knew he really would change ... There must be a gentler way to bring Harlan out of his shell. This seems so brutal.

Victor I have an idea — a much better idea. Yes — it may just work. (*Looking around*) This isn't the right place to discuss it, we could be overheard. Let's go for a walk, and I'll fill you in on all the details. But first, I should patch things up with Harlan.

Victor leads Colleen to the double doors

Meet me here in — (*looking at his watch*) exactly five minutes. Oh, and bring that lantern from the boathouse. It's pretty dark outside.

Colleen This isn't going to hurt him?

Victor Hurt him? No, no, no! This plan is gentleness itself. Why use vinegar when we have honey?

Colleen Honey?

Victor Come back in five minutes and all will be revealed. I just need time to apologize to Harlan.

Colleen All right. And thank you, Victor. (*She kisses him on the cheek*)

Colleen exits through the double doors

Victor picks up the pistol from the chess table, and looks around. He places the pistol carefully on top of the bar. Then he calls down the hallway where Harlan last exited

Victor Harlan! Harlan!

Harlan enters behind Victor through the double doors

Harlan I'm sorry about my outburst, Victor! I don't know what came over me.

Victor I'm sorry too. I went too far. I should never have mentioned Helen. You were right — it was all just a game ... I was testing you. I wanted to see how your philosophy held up under fire. I hope you'll forgive me.

Harlan All that you said about ... ?

Victor Just made it up as I went along.

Harlan Oh, thank heavens! That incident with the boy is such a fog in my mind, I don't know what's true and what isn't any more. Oh, Victor, you can be such a rogue sometimes! I do wish you'd stick to good old-fashioned debate.

Victor Debate is boring. It's also meaningless. Remember what you used to say: "True character is only revealed under stress."

Harlan Yes, I did say that, didn't I? Well, I've had enough stress for one night. Can we relax and get back to our game?

Victor Certainly.

They each pick up chess pieces

Can you remember where we were?

Harlan I think this was it. (*He puts some chess pieces on the board and sees the broken one*) Ah, this one's broken.

Victor Is it?

They sit on opposite sides of the chessboard and contemplate their next moves

I've been in a rotten mood all day. That's why I'm behaving the way I am. I think it's because I have something to get off my chest. You remember that old saying, "the truth shall make you free", and all that? Well, I want to be set free. I've been under a lot of strain recently. Dora has been — well, you know Dora — and I've hardly caught a fish since we've been here — and to cap it all I've been having an affair with your wife.

Harlan I see.

Beat

(*Still staring at the chessboard*) Yes, that can be quite a strain. Have you tried using a different bait?

Victor looks at Harlan

Victor I said, I've been having an affair with your wife. Colleen.

Harlan It's funny ... but, that's what I thought you said. (*He stares at the chessboard, goes to move a piece, then stops*)

Victor That's what I said.

Harlan What exactly do you mean by that?

Victor I mean I am having an affair with Colleen. Your wife. My mistress. Isn't that what it usually means?

Harlan That *is* what it usually means — but what did *you* mean?

Victor Let me try this again. I mean, your wife and I are sneaking around behind your back having sex. I mean, she is cheating on you, and I am cheating on Dora and we are both cheating together in the same bed. Our naked, sweaty bodies intertwine in a lustful frenzy. In a word, Harlan, we are f....

Harlan (*stopping Victor*) Yes ... Yes ... I think I get the picture.

Victor I get no pleasure telling you this, Harlan. The truth is, I've been wracked with guilt over it — so to save our friendship, I'm confessing everything and begging for your forgiveness.

Harlan Of course.

There is a silence. The two men stare at each other. Slowly Harlan starts to shake and his face contorts. Then he bursts out laughing

Oh, Victor! You never give up! Just when I think you're going to be serious, you're off pulling another stunt. You are a character! I can never tell what you're going to get up to next! (*He hoots with laughter*) Of course, you went too far with this Colleen thing. The reason I married Colleen was because she is the most honest, loyal human being I have ever met. I don't even have to think about infidelity with her! Can't fault you for trying, though, but I'm afraid it won't wash. You can't get me twice in a row! (*He laughs so hard he has to take his glasses off and wipe his eyes. He moves his chess piece*) By the way, I just took your queen! (*He howls with laughter*)

Victor She's meeting me right here in (*checking his watch*) — about two minutes.

This sets Harlan off laughing again; he continues to laugh through the following

We're going to make love out in the woods.

Harlan slaps his leg — it's all too funny

I asked her to meet me here once I got you out of the way. I've always loved the way she looks outside in the moonlight: virginal — uncorrupt — sacrificial. I just couldn't stop myself. You see, Harlan, women marry us men expecting we will change, but of course, we never do. And we foolish men — we marry a woman expecting she will never change, but of course, they always do. (*Bitterly*) They always change on us, Harlan.

Harlan holds his side; he is quite incapacitated with laughter

Harlan Oh, come on, Victor! You've had your fun. You got me all in a lather once. You should be satisfied.

Victor I'm sorry, Harlan. I'm truly sorry. (*He glances out of the window to see if Colleen is approaching. He indicates for Harlan to move into the corner behind the bar to hide*)

Harlan All right! I'll play along. But I'm going to get you back for all this, Victor. Be warned. (*He goes behind the bar*)

Victor turns off the main room lights, leaving only the light over the bar. Victor takes a candle from behind the bar, lights it, places it by the pistol, then settles in next to Harlan behind the bar — their heads still visible

Victor You know something, Harlan? Neither of us should have married. Nietzsche said that a married philosopher is a figure of comedy. The fact is, you've built your universe upon a false god, old friend. The "next world" is as much of a myth as Colleen's fidelity.
Harlan Are you suggesting a conjunctive proposition?
Victor Your doubt in one may lead to your doubt in the other.
Harlan It would. I am as sure of Colleen as I am that there is another plane of existence out there. They are both the northern stars of my belief.
Victor Then behold a cosmic collapse!

Victor pulls the cord to the hanging light over the bar, plunging the room into near darkness. The only light is the spill from the moonlight outside, and the candle illuminating the pistol. Harlan keeps chuckling to himself

Colleen enters on to the deck carrying a lantern

Colleen Victor! Victor!

Harlan stares at Colleen in shock. All his laughter drains from him

Victor You see, Harlan, we had arranged to make love under the stars while Dora was away this evening.

Colleen crosses the deck to the double doors with the lantern

Harlan No! It's quite impossible ... There's something missing — something I don't know!
Victor You still don't believe it, do you? Well, in the interests of truth, I'll prove it to you.

Colleen comes into the room through the double doors

Colleen Victor ? I'm ready. (*She peers into the darkness of the room*)
Victor (*going to Colleen*) Colleen.
Colleen Oh, there you are! It's so dark in here.

Victor and Colleen stand silhouetted in the moonlit frame of the open double doors. Suddenly Victor sweeps her into his arms and kisses her! This takes Colleen by such surprise that she does not resist for a moment

Colleen Mmmmm. ... Vict ... !

Victor keeps kissing her; Harlan watches with horror

Harlan Nooooooooooooooooooooooo!
Colleen (*pushing Victor away*) Oh, my God! Harlan!
Victor (*to Harlan*) Don't take it so hard, old pal. It's like I told you: to be a real seeker after truth, there has to be one terrible moment in your life when you doubt everything.
Harlan *You stinking son-of-a-bitch!* (*He grabs the pistol from the bar, aims it at Victor, and pulls the trigger*)

There is a loud blast from the pistol and Victor gets knocked backwards

Victor Hey! That hurt! (*He staggers a few steps, grasping on to some furniture*) Boy, yes — that really stung! (*Fighting to stay on his feet*) Something seems to have gone wron ... (*He stumbles around for a few more moments and then collapses*)

Harlan looks at the pistol in his hand with horror

Harlan My God! What have I done!

Colleen turns the lights back on and rushes to Victor's body. She opens his fisherman's vest and sees blood

Colleen You shot him right through the heart!
Harlan No!

Colleen puts her hand to Victor's neck to feel his pulse, and also listens for breathing

Colleen He's dead! Oh, dear God, he's dead!
Harlan He can't be! (*He goes to the body*) No! No! Victor ! My old friend! Why did you do it? You knew I'd pull the trigger! Why?
Colleen I don't understand ... He told me he'd put blanks in the gun — that he'd taken the real bullets out!
Harlan Blanks! So that's why he was waving the gun in front of my face all night! I should have known it was one of his perverted games!
Colleen He must have left a bullet in by accident! Oh, no — no! Oh, God! This is all my fault! I should have told you! I should have told you!
Harlan How could I have been so stupid?
Colleen He asked me to meet him here so we could talk. Talk about you, Harlan! I never expected him to kiss me like that!
Harlan It doesn't matter what happened! Nothing matters any more! A lifetime of reason and reflection, and I end up — a common murderer. So, it's true. I can kill someone. Maybe he's right about everything. We are just animals. I was wrong — I was wrong! (*He sighs*) I'll call the police.

Colleen The police!
Harlan Of course — I've murdered him.
Colleen It wasn't murder! I told you, it was an accident!
Harlan For him, maybe, but not for me. When I pulled that trigger I wanted nothing more than to see him dead!
Colleen You don't have to tell the police that!
Harlan What else can I tell them?
Colleen Just tell them ... Oh, God, I don't know! How did I get us into this nightmare?
Harlan It's all right, Colleen. It was entirely my fault. I had a choice and I made it. In my own way I'm just as dead as poor Victor over there. (*He goes to the phone*) Let's get this over with.
Colleen No! Wait!

Harlan stops

This was not murder, Harlan! It was a prank that went wrong! It was an accident! He provoked you! (*Pointing angrily at Victor*) It was *his* fault for not checking the gun more carefully.
Harlan An interesting point. I'll debate it with the judge. I'll confess to everything and throw myself on the mercy of the court. (*He winces*) Oh, no ... The Tomlins incident is bound to come up. I'm a menace to society, no doubt about that. It's a shame they don't hang people any more!
Colleen *Stop it! Stop it!* I'm the one responsible for this! If I'd just told you, it would never have happened. And your going to jail won't bring Victor back to life! What about us? I love you! You can't just throw that all away!
Harlan I love you too, Colleen.
Colleen You do? Really?
Harlan (*holding her tenderly*) By every definition there ever was. (*Abruptly*) But it's too late to think about that now. (*He starts to dial the telephone*)
Colleen Wait! We can still work out a story!
Harlan A story?
Colleen (*excitedly*) We'll tell them it was an accident. You weren't arguing about anything. You were just playing with the gun (*picking up the pistol*) — joking — everybody in a good mood. (*She waves the gun around wildly like someone who's never handled a gun before*)

Whenever the gun points towards Harlan, he ducks down behind the bar

Nobody thought the gun was loaded ... It just went off ...
Harlan Colleen! The gun! Be careful!
Colleen (*frantically*) It happens all the time!
Harlan But it didn't happen this time!

Colleen (*desperately*) Nobody has to know that!
Harlan The police would see right through it.
Colleen Not if we have a plan!
Harlan Please — the gun ...!
Colleen Right now, you and I are the only ones that know!
Harlan I won't be involved with any more lies. (*He starts to dial again*)
Colleen *Stop right there!* (*She points the pistol directly at Harlan*)
Harlan What do you think you're doing?
Colleen I'm not going to let you do it!
Harlan (*looking at Colleen with astonishment*) I'm not sure if you've thought this all the way through.
Colleen *Put ... the ... phone ... down!*

Harlan studies her for a moment, thinks about putting the phone down, then changes his mind and dials. Colleen aims the pistol at him throughout the following

Harlan (*into the phone*) Hello, is that the police? I want to report a shooting.
Colleen I'll use this if I have to!
Harlan (*into the phone*) No, I don't think that'll be necessary. He's dead.
Colleen I'm warning you! Don't tell them another word!
Harlan (*into the phone*) We don't have a street address — we're in a cottage on Matagami Inlet ... We're the wooden one with a chimney ...
Colleen I'm ordering you for the last time — (*going over the edge*) *put that phone down!*
Harlan (*into the phone*) No, I knew the deceased man very well. He was my best friend. ... My name? Prof...

Colleen pulls the trigger and shoots. She hits the base of the telephone which flies off and lands on the floor behind the bar. Harlan still holds the receiver in his hand, and looks down in shock as he sees the wire dangling uselessly in the air

Colleen They didn't hear your name — we can still work something out!
Harlan (*staring at Colleen, astonished*) Colleen! This is not the woman I married!
Colleen *You bet your ass it isn't!* If you won't look after yourself, then I'll have to do it for you!

Car headlights flash across the window

There's a car coming! Maybe it's the police!
Harlan Someone must have heard the shots.

There is a rumble of thunder

Colleen The body!
Harlan The body?
Colleen The body! We have to hide it!
Harlan Why? I'm going to tell them the truth!
Colleen (*losing what little patience she has left*) We'll — hide — the — body — until — they — go!
Harlan No, Colleen! I'm drawing the line right here!

Colleen aims the pistol right at Harlan's head! She looks crazed and out of control

Where do you want it?
Colleen In our bedroom, over there!

Harlan drags Victor's body towards the bedroom. Colleen keeps the pistol aimed at him. She looks out of the window

Harlan This is crazy — crazy!
Colleen Faster! They're coming up the path!

Harlan is having trouble — the body is heavy and awkward

Move it!

Colleen tosses the telephone receiver behind the bar. She quickly hides the pistol behind the bar, blows out the candle, then grabs a bottle of brandy and starts guzzling it

Harlan gets Victor's body into the bedroom, steps out of the room and slams the door closed

Dora enters through the double doors at the exact moment the door slams

Colleen Oh! It's you!

Harlan casually takes a book from the bookshelf and sits, pretending to read

Dora Hi, Colleen. Harlan.

There is another rumble of thunder

Sounds like a storm brewing.

Dora puts her umbrella away, looking around, eagle-eyed. She senses something has gone on. Colleen takes another big swig of brandy, which Dora notices

Dora Where's Victor?

Suddenly the double doors explode open and Officer McGuire leaps into the room — gun drawn

Everyone leaps back in terror. Harlan's book goes flying into the air

Officer McGuire Freeze! Get your hands in the air!

The others look at her, stunned. Harlan goes to pick up his book, but Officer McGuire stomps on it with her boot and puts her gun in Harlan's face

I said, get your hands in the air!
Dora What for?
Officer McGuire Never mind what for! Just do it!

Officer McGuire looks more than a bit dangerous, so the others quickly raise their hands. She frisks them during the following

We just got a report of a gunshot from a cottager across the bay.
Dora A gunshot? How very curious.
Colleen Nobody's been shooting anyone here. It's been a very quiet evening.
Officer McGuire Your neighbour heard a loud argument going on here, and then a gunshot. Naturally he called the police. (*She finishes frisking them, and then holsters her gun*) All right! Why don't you tell me what's been going on here? You can put your hands down. (*She flips out her notebook*)

Colleen knocks back another mouthful of brandy

Officer McGuire (*to Colleen*) Your name?
Colleen Mrs Harlan Brandstater. (*Drunkenly friendly*) But you can call me Colleen.
Officer McGuire (*writing*) Mrs Brandstater. Have you been in all evening?
Colleen Yes, I have.
Officer McGuire (*to Harlan*) And your name, sir?
Harlan Har...
Colleen (*interrupting*) His name's Harlan Brandstater. (*She moves to Harlan's side*) Professor Harlan Brandstater. He's my husband. Teaches philosophy at U.B.C. He specializes in the Stoics — you know, the peaceful, non-violent approach to life. And he was in all evening too.
Officer McGuire (*to Harlan*) Is that correct?

Colleen Yes.

Officer McGuire (*to Colleen, sarcastically*) You don't mind me asking your husband a few questions, I hope?

Colleen Of course not. We have nothing to hide. (*Sternly*) Do we, Harlan?

Officer McGuire Thank you so much. (*To Harlan*) Are you the owner of the handgun I saw earlier?

Colleen No, that's Victor's.

Officer McGuire Victor?

Colleen Professor Victor Pierce. Dora's husband.

Officer McGuire And where is he?

Colleen and Harlan exchange glances; Officer McGuire notices this

Colleen
Harlan } (*together*) Out.

Officer McGuire makes a note in her book about what she's seen

Officer McGuire Professor Brandstater, did you hear any shots in this vicinity?

Harlan starts to say something

Colleen Oh, I remember! Yes! Now I know what you're talking about! That wasn't a shot — it was the propane stove in the kitchen. The oven igniter doesn't work properly — every so often it goes off with a boom. (*To Harlan*) We really should get that fixed.

Officer McGuire So you were cooking?

Colleen That's right.

Officer McGuire looks around but sees no sign of a meal

Officer McGuire I don't smell any food.

Colleen It's all gone. Delicious, if I may say so.

Officer McGuire And where did you say this Professor Pierce had gone?

There is another rumble of thunder, louder this time

(*Seeing something on the floor*) Wait a minute — what's that?

Colleen What?

Officer McGuire There! On the floor. That looks like drops of blood!

Colleen That's impossible!

Officer McGuire gets down on one knee and stares at the red drops

Officer McGuire Yes. It's blood! (*She leaps up, instinctively whips out her gun and rather idiotically aims it right at the drops of blood. Seeing that she's aiming at the wrong thing, she wheels around and aims it at Harlan and Colleen*) *Stand back!* (*She sees another drop*) Aha! There's more drops! They seem to be leading towards this door ... (*She follows the blood trail to the bedroom and moves to open the door*)

Colleen (*leaping in front of Officer McGuire*) *Don't look in there!*

Officer McGuire (*stopping*) And why not, Mrs Brandstater?

Colleen (*after a pause*) It's a mess!

Harlan (*realizing the gig is up*) Oh, God ... !

Officer McGuire Mrs Brandstater, this is an investigation of a shooting — possibly even murder.

Dora Murder?

Officer McGuire If you're trying to protect somebody ...

Colleen (*giving up*) All right! I confess!

Harlan (*coming forward*) That's enough, Colleen! Let me get this off my chest!

Officer McGuire I'll take both your statements right after I see what's in here ...

Officer McGuire opens the bedroom door, gun drawn and poised to shoot. She rushes inside and exits

As Officer McGuire goes there is a sudden flash of lightning and crack of thunder. The double doors blow open

Victor enters through the double doors in a shroud of mist. His face is just a shade lighter than usual, and his entrance has an eerie spectral quality to it

Harlan sees Victor and screams! Dora and Colleen turn to look at Victor. Colleen faints. Victor looks around to see what everyone is staring at

Victor What's going on? What's the matter? You all look like you've seen a ghost!

There is another violent flash of lightning and the sound of a gust of wind which rattles the entire cottage

Colleen revives, points a horrified finger at Victor and faints again

The Lights fade

Music

ACT II

The same. Just a few seconds later

Victor is still standing in the double doorway shrouded in mist

Harlan helps Colleen get up from her faint

There is another flicker of lightning followed by a rumble of thunder

Victor Are you all right, Colleen?
Colleen Yes! I — must have a touch of the flu or something.

Harlan helps Colleen over to a chair. She fans herself and sits down

Officer McGuire comes out of the bedroom looking confused

Officer McGuire What the heck ... (*She sees Victor and points her gun at him*) Who are you?
Harlan This is Professor Pierce.
Officer McGuire (*disappointed*) Oh. (*She holsters her gun*)

Victor moves DS *but his gait is clumsy, as if his legs are having trouble holding him up. He seems in a bit of a daze*

Victor (*cheerfully*) Hello, officer! Hot on the trail of the tricycle thief, are you?
Officer McGuire Actually, I've been wondering where you were, Professor. (*She whips out her notebook and writes throughout the following*)
Victor Really?
Dora Are you feeling all right, Victor? You look a bit pale.
Victor Yes, I'm fine. I must have fallen asleep down by the beach — that thunder woke me up. You know, I had a most extraordinary dream — it was weird. I was going down this long path with a gate at the end of it ... It was beautiful, but I felt this pain in my chest. I was about to go through the gate when I heard voices shouting. I turned and saw Harlan and Colleen, yelling to me, "Stop! It was all an accident!" I saw Dora there too, but you didn't say anything. Suddenly somebody screamed, "Don't look in there!". I stepped back, and *blam*, the gate slammed shut in front of me. Then I woke up.

The others stare at him

Well, I told you it was weird.

Officer McGuire stops writing in her notebook

Officer McGuire Guess I can't arrest anyone for having a bad dream — even a dream as stupid as that. (*Turning to Colleen*) So what were you going to confess, Mrs Brandstater?
Colleen What?
Officer McGuire Before I went into that bedroom you said you wanted to confess.
Colleen Oh! That ... That ... I forgot to make the bed.
Officer McGuire You forgot to make the bed?
Colleen I know, I know, it's terrible! I took a nap this afternoon and since we weren't expecting visitors ... (*In anguish*) Oh God ... I just didn't do it! (*She bursts into tears*)
Officer McGuire Calm down! I can't arrest you for that either. (*Turning to Harlan*) And what were you going to get off your chest, Professor Brandstater?
Harlan (*still staring at Victor in shock*) Did I have something to get off my chest?
Officer McGuire Yes, you did. Something seemed to be weighing on your conscience.
Harlan My conscience has been healed. It's a miracle!
Officer McGuire What? Just now?
Colleen That lightning strike must have created a cosmic energy field. (*To Officer McGuire*) Didn't you feel the healing power of nature?
Harlan Hallelujah!
Officer McGuire Are you some kind of religious cult?
Colleen No. (*Prancing about*) We just worship the trees and the plants and the sky and the clouds and all the little crawling creatures ...
Officer McGuire All right, all right! I don't care about any of that.
Dora (*looking at Victor closely*) Are you sure you're feeling all right, Victor? You don't look at all well to me.
Victor I do feel a bit light-headed. I shouldn't have eaten that piece of cheese after lunch. (*He moves awkwardly to the armchair and plops down*)
Officer McGuire There's something very odd going on here. Is there anyone else staying here besides you four?
Dora That's it, Officer. No corpses, I'm afraid.

Officer McGuire looks suspiciously at the blood on the floor again. Colleen gets her box of paints

Colleen I must have spilled some paint. (*She shows the box to Officer McGuire*) See!

Officer McGuire (*sadly ripping the pages out of her notebook*) Ah well! I'll go over and question the cottager who made the report.

Officer McGuire exits. After a beat she enters

And another thing. Clear the damn brush around this cottage!

She exits

Dora looks closely at Victor. He picks up a newspaper, then notices Dora staring at him

Victor Is anything wrong? You look disappointed about something, dearest.

Dora No, no! The lecture wasn't as good as I had hoped.

Victor Oh? The one about "Men Who Are... ?" (*He seems forgetful*)

Dora "Pigs". It seems that kind of man is very hard to get rid of. (*She scrutinizes Victor*)

Harlan Well ... Now that all the excitement is over, I think I'll — (*he looks at Colleen questioningly: what do they do now?*) finish my new course outline.

Colleen looks back at Victor. Dora notices their exchange of looks. Harlan crosses the room, but his gaze is fastened on Victor

Dora (*to Victor*) So, you're feeling absolutely fine?

Victor Yes! I've already told you, it's probably something I ate. Nothing serious.

Dora Are you sure you don't want me to check you out?

Victor Yes, I'm sure!

Dora It wouldn't take a minute ... (*She picks up her doctor's bag and takes out the stethoscope. She looks into Victor's eyes — doing a medical examination*)

Victor Damn it, Dora! There's nothing wrong with me! You've been reading too many medical books. I know you'd love to shove your thermometers and sphygmomanometers up all my orifices, but I happen to be perfectly healthy.

Dora I'm just concerned about your welfare, dearest.

Victor I simply want to put my feet up and relax. Go practise medicine on someone else! (*He goes back to his newspaper*)

Dora moves away from Victor, putting her bag down with the stethoscope protruding. There is an uncomfortable silence. Harlan flicks through a book, although he is obviously not reading it. Colleen flits nervously, looking for something to do

Colleen (*shrilly*) Coffee, anyone? Harlan?
Harlan Er ... Sure!
Colleen Victor?
Victor No, thanks.
Colleen What about you, Dora?
Dora No, thanks. (*She picks up her books*) I think I'll go down to the boathouse and do some studying.
Colleen (*overeagerly*) What a good idea!
Harlan Yes! A very good idea! (*He dashes to the double doors and opens them for Dora*) We'll just stay and hold the fort — and you can — study away!

Dora looks closely at the others

Dora I'll probably be a while. Don't wait up.

Dora exits

Victor tosses the newspaper aside, gets up and looks around

Victor Have you seen my "Fish Facts Monthly"? The one with the article about "Boating That Big-Mouth Bass".
Harlan I think I saw it — out on the deck!

Victor unsteadily leaves the room through the double doors. He can be seen looking around for the magazine on the deck, staggering clumsily back and forth, during the following

(*Whispering*) Oh, my God! They sent him back!
Colleen (*whispering*) He must be in some kind of limbo!
Harlan I think you're right.
Colleen But why? Why does anyone get stuck in limbo?
Harlan I don't know — it's really not my field.
Colleen We have to do something for him! Maybe it's this house! No! The mask! The spirits of the Nootka are angry with us and won't let him go! This is all my fault! I must have used the wrong chants!
Harlan Stop trying to take the blame for this! I shot him!

Colleen Well, we can't just let him wander around like this! You must talk to him!

Harlan What could I tell him? I've never even seen a ghost before, and now I'm supposed to sit one down and give it some advice!

Colleen It's not just any ghost! It's Victor!

Harlan I don't know what to say to him!

Colleen You're a philosophy professor! Surely there's something...

Harlan It's not that easy! I've studied life, and I've studied death, but this is — neither!

Victor sticks his nose up against the screen window

Victor Are you sure you saw it on the deck?

Harlan Yes.

Victor goes back to lurching around the deck

Colleen (*to Harlan*) There must be something in one of your books about it!

Harlan Yes! That's possible! I did bring some of my reference books ... (*He rushes to the bookshelf*) Evans-Pritchard ... Middleton ... No ... No ... (*He pulls a book out*) Aha! This may have something ... (*Flicking through the book*) Ghosts—phantoms—poltergeists ... Here we are: "The Relationship Between The Spirit And The Body". (*He scans the text*) Hmmm. There must be something about situations like these ... (*Reading*) "The sighting of a spirit after burial ..." No — that's not ... Ah, here we are — listen to this: (*reading*) "There have been many reported instances of a corpse transmogrifying straight into a spirit. These cases leave no visible corpse because the body becomes the spectre, and during the night-time hours the spectre can walk abroad as a human ... " etc, etc. (*Reading*) "Such was the famous case of Sir Robert Banastre of Passenham ... "

Victor (*calling out from the deck, holding up the magazine*) Found it! You were right! (*He sits on a chair outside on the deck with his back to them and reads. During the following, piqued by Colleen's and Harlan's whispering, he gets up and looks through the screen window at them*)

Colleen (*whispering to Harlan*) Does it say why they become spirits? Is there anything we can do?

Harlan Hmm. Let me see ... (*He scans the page; reading*) "Transcendental dialectics and theology ..." Here, here — this could be it! (*Reading*) "Some experts, such as Hofmeister and Rhees-Jones, theorize that the powers of light and the powers of darkness are still fighting for possession of the soul! In such cases, though the ghost is unaware of his ectoplasmic state, his actions during this time can influence the final outcome of that battle."

Colleen You mean it hasn't been decided whether he goes — (*she indicates "up"*) or — (*she indicates "down"*).
Harlan Exactly.
Colleen Poor Victor!
Harlan You're right, we have to help him somehow.
Colleen He doesn't even know he's dead.
Harlan We're going to have to break the news to him. (*Wincing*) Oh, dear! All those affairs he's had must be getting him into hot water right now. Apart from that he's led a pretty good life. If we can convince him that he's dead, perhaps he can reconcile with Dora, and that may put him over the top with — er — You-Know-Who ...

Harlan sees Victor staring at them through the screen

He's heard us! Let me talk to him. The sooner we break the news to him, the better chance he'll have.
Colleen Are you sure you want to do it alone?
Harlan It'll be less of a shock coming from an old friend.
Colleen You're right. I'll try some different chants. He needs all the help he can get. (*She turns to leave*)
Harlan Colleen! I'm sorry I didn't trust you. I was such a fool. You must think very little of me now.
Colleen It only proves you're human, that's all. (*In tears*) Not like poor Victor.

Colleen exits through the hallway

Victor comes in through the double doors with the magazine as Colleen goes

Victor What were you two whispering about so earnestly? (*He scratches himself*) Damn! I think I got bitten by fire ants when I was sleeping.

Harlan paces for a moment, not knowing where to start

Harlan Victor ... ?
Victor Yes?
Harlan Aaah ... (*He loses his nerve*) Would you — like a brandy?
Victor No thanks.
Harlan Well, I need one. (*He gets the bottle of brandy from the bar. He is about to pour a glass when instead he just grabs the bottle and swigs down a stiff shot*) So, Victor — (*the effect of the brandy kicks in*) haaaargh! (*He

recovers) This dream you had — can you remember anything more about it? You say there was a gate ...

Victor Yes.

Harlan A big gate?

Victor Medium-sized.

Harlan Made of wood?

Victor Yes. Why are you asking me all these questions? (*Sarcastically*) I suppose you're going to tell me this dream had some deep psychological significance?

Harlan Not psychological, no. It's just very interesting, don't you think? Both Christian and Eastern religions talk about a gate. The Pearly Gates ... The Vedic scriptures of India talk about your soul passing through a gate ... The shamans of the Lakota Sioux Indians refer to a Spirit Gate to welcome the dead ...

Victor What's your point, Harlan?

Harlan My point is — this dream could be a symbol — a pointer — a representation of your present state.

Victor (*shrugging*) It's only a dream!

Harlan Perhaps not! I mean — let's examine that! For example — do you recall what you were doing before you die... umm — fell asleep?

Victor It's funny, but I don't remember much of this afternoon at all.

Harlan Nothing?

Victor Fishing! I remember fishing!

Harlan Do you remember — a gun?

Victor A gun? Yes. My point 44 Magnum. What about it?

Harlan It went off.

Victor Did it?

Harlan At you.

Victor I see.

Harlan With a bullet in it. A real bullet.

Victor Ah.

Harlan (*pacing nervously*) I'm not sure quite how to put this, Victor, but I think you ought to know ... I mean, you are my closest friend — or were, would be a bit more accurate — so I think that it is my duty to tell you — er ...

Victor What are you drivelling about?

Harlan The fact is, Victor — (*taking a deep breath*) you're dead.

Beat

Victor It's true. I am feeling a bit lethargic.

Harlan No, Victor ! Dead! As in "dodo".

Victor You don't have to go on about it! I can't be the life and soul of the party all the time! You're not exactly Mr Lively yourself.

Harlan (*getting frustrated*) I am not using that term in a metaphorical sense, but literally, as in deceased, passed on — no longer with us! (*He mimes strangling himself and expiring*)

Victor Ah! That kind of dead. (*Beat*) Did I miss something? Who was it you said had — (*mimicking Harlan's mime-show*) passed on?

Harlan *You!* Except you don't seem to have passed on at all. You're still here.

Victor (*looking at himself*) I'm definitely still here.

Harlan Victor ! I know you're dead because — I was the one who killed you!

Victor Oh! That seems a little unfriendly, Harlan, if you don't mind me saying so. Why did you do that?

Harlan I thought you were seducing Colleen. I had a little fit of jealousy. Quite unforgivable.

Victor Seducing Colleen? (*He smiles as he remembers*) Ah, yes — and you took ——

Harlan — your gun ——

Victor — and shot me. Yes ... Yes ... It's beginning to come back ...

Harlan Apparently there was supposed to be a blank in the gun.

Victor Yes! That's right! A blank! I remember that! (*Beat*) What do you mean "apparently"?

Harlan There was a mistake. A *big* mistake.

Victor (*looking closely at Harlan*) You're not serious, are you? (*Laughing*) I do believe you are! And now you think I'm a ghost. (*Looking into Harlan's eyes*) You do, don't you? Harlan — my poor, poor Harlan. That superstitious logic of yours has finally driven you off the deep end, hasn't it? (*He jokingly extends his arms and moves zombie-like towards Harlan*) Look at me! Touch me! I'm flesh and blood! I'm perfectly all right.

Harlan backs away in fear, falling over the furniture

Harlan Now, I know it must be a little disconcerting at first, but try to look on the bright side! Think what we've discovered here! If you could hang on a little longer — if we could document this — it could change the way we all think about ourselves! The eternal fight between faith and reason — between cosmological dialectics and hard science — could be over! Think of what it means!

Victor It means you're going nuts, that's what it means! I think I will have that brandy.

Victor goes to the bar and pours himself a stiff shot

Colleen can be heard chanting off stage

What the hell's that? (*He looks out of the window*) Oh, it's Colleen. Isn't it a bit late for her to be doing her chants?

Harlan Let's hope not! You're in limbo, Victor! You have become what the old alchemists called a "Spiritus Mercurialis", the much sought-after corporeal connection to the afterlife! Now that I'm getting over the shock of killing you, I'm beginning to realize that this could be the most amazing discovery in history! We have to put this in its academic perspective. (*Excitedly*) I don't believe my luck! (*He grabs a large notepad and pencil from a shelf*)

Victor I think you've got one of your wheels caught in the sand, Harlan.

Colleen's off stage chanting fades during the following

Harlan (*beside himself with excitement*) "Arcanum arcanorum!" The secret of secrets! It's within our grasp! We have been given an opportunity to conduct the world's first physico-ephemeral experiment! (*He checks his watch and writes the date and time at the top of the page*) There's a good possibility that your fate is being decided *as we speak!* Now, I think it all hinges on cleaning up the — shall we say — negative aspects of your life. You can't change the past, but there is something you could change before you go — you could reconcile with Dora! If you did that I think you'd stand a much better chance ...

Victor Oh, do shut up! I had a bizarre dream ... I forgot a couple of things for a moment — it doesn't mean I'm a half-decomposed zombie who's just crawled out of his grave, for heaven's sake!

Harlan Victor, I don't want you to think that I'm not sorry that I killed you — I am. I should have been able to control myself. My life's work has been the quest to curb anger and passion, and you set me a glorious test — it was brilliant — I commend you. You exploited my weaknesses like a master! As a human being I was an abject failure — yet, at the same time — you must admit, my philosophy ... My philosophy was a magnificent success!

Victor Success! Ha! I'd like to see how you can pull success out of the philosophical trouncing I just gave you!

Harlan Victor, Victor! Don't you see? I have proven ... We have proven — beyond a shadow of doubt — that there *is* life after death! This changes everything! (*He excitedly scribbles down notes*)

Victor You haven't proven any such thing! It was a game! I was trying to prove a point! Those weren't real bullets in the gun — they were blanks! Get it? Blanks! *You didn't kill me!*

Harlan I did! I shot you right through the heart!

Victor OK, if I'm dead, there should be a bullet hole in my vest, shouldn't there? (*He looks at his vest, which has no hole in it*) Well?

Harlan Wait! You had your hands in your pant pockets — your vest was pulled aside.

Victor Then I should have a bullet hole in my shirt, shouldn't I? (*He opens his vest; his shirt has a large round bloodstain around the area of his heart. He convulses in horror when he sees the stain*)

Harlan (*hopping around in joy; gleefully*) You see! You see! Isn't it wonderful!

Victor No! No, no — no! (*He quickly closes his vest over the bloodstain*)

Harlan Go on, Victor — look at it. You could probably stick your finger right through the hole. (*He moves his finger towards Victor's chest*)

Victor (*jumping back with squeamish horror, buttoning up his vest*) Get away from me!

Harlan Just as I thought — you can't face your own mortality, can you?

Victor Oh, no ... Forget it, Harlan! I'm not buying your little ruse! You can't catch me as easily as that! You're getting back at me because of what I did to you! Aha — that's it, isn't it? Isn't it?

Harlan No, Victor ! You must face up to the facts! You're in denial. Remember Kübler-Ross's theory of the five stages of dying? The first stage is denial, then comes anger, then bargaining for time ——

Victor (*losing his confidence*) Come on, Harlan! Out with it! Your scheme has been discovered! How did you get the blood there? Some sleight of hand? Very clever, but I know what you're up to! Come on, tell me! You want me to admit that there is an afterlife, don't you? You just want to hear me say, "Yes, there is life after death — I was wrong, you were right," and then everyone will come prancing out shouting, "We got you — we got you!" (*Looking around*) Well, the game's over! No-one's making a damn fool out of Victor Pierce, and that's the end of it! Come on — you can all come out! (*He opens the double doors and looks out. After a silence*) I'm not dead!

Harlan To understand the truth there has to be one terrible moment in your life when you doubt everything. Isn't that what you said?

Victor You bastard! You don't play games with people's lives!

Harlan You did with mine!

Victor You've concocted this elaborate hoax because I proved that you were capable of murder! And you hate being proved wrong, don't you?

Harlan Not as much as you do, Victor.

Victor A red stain on my shirt proves nothing! It could be ketchup, or paint! You snuck up on me while I was asleep down at the beach, didn't you? That's it, isn't it? Yes! Of course! (*Laughing with relief*) You had me worried for a moment — I don't mind admitting it! But I've got it all figured out now! Ketchup! Ha! (*Looking at the stain and breathing more easily*) And that gate in the dream ... It was just like that gate by the boathouse — yeah, that old wooden gate — no Pearly Gates there! (*He looks even more relieved and scratches himself*) Damned itch! It's driving me nuts.

Harlan It's your skin! It's beginning to decompose. (*He grabs his notepad, checks the time on his watch and scribbles down more notes*)

Victor *Stop it!* It's fire ants and ketchup!

Harlan We need something more scientific to prove you're dead. (*He looks around and sees the large mercury thermometer on the wall; he grabs it and goes to Victor*) Open wide!

Harlan tries to put the thermometer in Victor's mouth, but with its wooden backing it's obviously too big

Victor What the hell are you doing?

Harlan Taking your temperature.

Victor That's not going to work, you idiot!

Harlan You're right. (*He looks around and sees the stethoscope hanging out of Dora's medical bag*) Ah! Look, Dora's stethoscope!

Victor Yes! Dora's stethoscope! This will put an end to this stupid notion of yours once and for all! (*He grabs the stethoscope*) Let's take a listen to the old ticker. (*He clips the stethoscope on his ears, puts the sensor against his chest and listens*) This'll show you! You can't have a ghost with a heartbeat, can you? (*His face turns from triumph to concern*) Hmm. This thing doesn't work too well. Battery must be flat.

Harlan It doesn't use a battery.

Victor scowls and moves the sensor around his chest — slowly at first, and then more desperately

Victor There must be some mistake! I ... I can't hear anything.

Harlan Of course you can't hear anything. There's no blood pumping through your veins.

Victor Damn it! What's the matter with this stupid thing! (*He jabs the sensor all over his chest, then at the pulse point of the wrist. Nothing! Finally he jams it against the carotid artery of the neck. Still nothing*)

Harlan It's as silent as a tomb, isn't it?

Victor (*ripping off the stethoscope and hurling it across the room*) No! It can't be true! It can't be!

Harlan It is, Victor!

Victor No! No! No! Oh, I don't feel so good!

Harlan I'm sorry, Victor. I'm truly sorry.

Victor This is worse than being told you're terminally ill! You're saying I'm …

Harlan Beyond terminal. Beyond everything. Simply and unequivocally dead!

Victor (*slumping down on to a chair*) I'm dead! (*Whimpering*) I'm not prepared for this! Oh, I took a course in it once, but I fell asleep in half the lectures. That's it then! The end of everything! Oh no! (*He reacts to seeing something in his mind*)

Harlan What is it?

Victor I'm seeing my life flash before my eyes! It's true what they say! I can see myself as a child — playing in the yard — school — baseball — that home run I hit that won us the MacIntosh Challenge Cup! Yes! Yes! Now I'm a teenager — the day I wrecked the car — Dad's face, oh shit ... Ah —

and there's Dora — the senior prom ... (*Fondly*) Aaah, she looked so cute ... College — Harlan, it's you, it's you! It's the day we climbed the clock tower and hung a bra and panties on the clock hands ... (*He laughs raucously at the memory*) Oh, what fun we had ... Oh-oh — now it's three years ago! Oh no, I can't watch this ...

Harlan I know this must be very hard on you, but I had to tell you that there was a real bullet in that gun.

Victor (*almost in tears*) But Harlan, how did it happen? How? There shouldn't have been a bullet in the gun!

Harlan But there was, and that's the end of it! You must have left a bullet in the chamber by accident!

Victor I didn't leave a bullet in by accident! I'm not that stupid! (*Realizing*) Somebody else must have put the bullet there!

Harlan That's ridiculous! Why would anybody do that?

Victor (*his self-pity turning to anger*) Somebody who wanted me dead!

Harlan Nobody wanted you dead! It was an accident!

Victor No, Harlan! I checked that gun very carefully! I was murdered!

Harlan Yes! I murdered you! I'm ready to confess to it. But I can't while you're still here. The police need a corpse, and nobody's going to give you a death certificate while you're sitting around reading "Fish Facts Monthly".

Victor I'm not talking about you, you dope! I wanted you to shoot me! But someone switched the bullets in the gun! Someone knew about the game and switched the bullets! But who?

Harlan Never mind how it happened! It's not important now! You should be thinking about the time you have left — about saying goodbye to the people you love. You could start by reconciling with Dora — it could really help your case ...

Victor Dora! Yes! Maybe she did it ... She found out about the game and ...! (*He pauses thoughtfully*) No, she's just not the type. Besides, she takes enough tranquillizers to pacify a tiger. I need to find the person who would stand to gain the most from my death. Someone whose life — or whose career — (*it starts to make sense*) would be greatly improved with me out of the way. (*He glares at Harlan*) Someone whose course attendances have been declining for several years, because another professor is more popular. Someone who's just behind me in line for tenure. Can you think of anyone like that, Harlan?

Harlan Victor — you're not serious... ?

Victor (*approaching Harlan menacingly*) Colleen told you about the game, didn't she? And you realized that it would be easy to claim I had left the bullet in by mistake. It would all be dismissed as a little mishap! You could say it was — *a hunting accident! Yes!* And then you would be next in line for tenure! My God, what a fool I've been! I even put the thought into your head! I see it all now! *You* planned my murder!

Harlan That's ridiculous! You're my best friend!

Victor Friendship is never worth as much as tenure — you know that! It makes perfect sense! Finally I see you as you really are! *You're a murderer! A cold-blooded murderer!!* (*He looks around and sees the large wood-chopper's axe next to the woodpile. He heads for it*)

Harlan What are you doing?

Victor (*picking up the axe*) Revenge, Harlan! I want revenge! (*He approaches Harlan with the axe*)

Harlan Take it easy, Victor! It's just a phase you're going through! Remember Kübler-Ross and the five stages of dying? First denial, and then anger ...

Victor chases Harlan. Harlan trips and falls over the back of the sofa. Victor swings the axe at Harlan, who rolls away; the axe misses and thumps into the sofa

I'll be really glad when this stage is over! (*He runs across the room towards the chess table*)

Victor (*in hot pursuit*) I had a life — I had a future! And you took it all away from me!

Harlan But you do have a future! Maybe not on this earth, but it's still a future, of sorts!

Victor *Thanks for nothing!*

Victor swings the axe at Harlan again. It misses but impales the chessboard to the tree stump it is placed on. Chess pieces go flying everywhere! Victor tries to pull the axe out of the stump; Harlan wrestles with him for possession of the axe

Harlan This has all gone too far, Victor! It's time to take a couple of deep breaths and calm down.

Victor Thanks to you, I don't have any deep breaths to take! (*He gives up trying to pull the axe out of the stump. He sees the harpoon on the wall, grabs it and turns on Harlan*)

Harlan Victor !

Victor This is rather fitting, don't you think? A harpoon! Like Captain Ahab and the whale, we both go down together ... (*He hurls the harpoon at Harlan*)

Harlan dives to one side and the harpoon misses him. Victor returns to the axe and tries to pull it out of the table

Harlan uses the moment to rush into the bedroom L, *slamming the door behind him*

Victor frees the axe and runs to the door. Victor hears the sound of Harlan apparently locking the door and stops. He backs away to get a good run, puts his shoulder down and charges the bedroom door

Just as Victor reaches the door, Harlan pulls it open from inside and Victor goes flying through it; he can be heard tumbling over the furniture off stage. Harlan darts out of the door, closes it, rushes into the centre of the room, looks around, and then escapes through the bedroom door R

Victor emerges from the bedroom L *with the axe, but Harlan has disappeared. Victor runs to the double doors and exits into the foliage*

Colleen rushes in from the hallway

Colleen What's going on in here? Harlan? Victor ? (*She looks around the room at the upturned furniture and the harpoon*) Oh, my God!

Harlan enters US, *sprinting across the deck; he comes in through the double doors*

Harlan Colleen, get out of here! Victor's gone mad! He's on a rampage!

Victor enters US, *coming along the path to the deck, axe at the ready*

Harlan and Colleen turn and see Victor approaching

He's coming! Quick! Hide!

They look around in a panic. There's no time to hide so they press themselves against the wall on either side of the screen window. Victor arrives on the deck and stands framed in the window with his axe. He peers into the room through the screen. For a terrifying moment it seems that Victor senses their presence

The sound of rustling leaves comes from the woods

Victor hears the leaves rustling, turns and races off into the darkness

Colleen Harlan, what did you say to him? You were supposed to make him feel better.

Harlan I just told him he was dead. He didn't take it very well.

Victor comes back into view outside and starts prodding the shrubs with his axe looking for Harlan

Colleen and Harlan watch Victor nervously. Finding nothing, Victor comes back on the deck, looking around

Colleen He's coming back!

Harlan and Colleen hide, Harlan behind the bar, Colleen behind some furniture

Victor comes in through the double doors, the axe poised

Victor Where are you, Harlan? (*Looking around*) Harlan? There's no point in running! I'm going to get you! I'm not going into the great beyond alone!

Victor reacts to hearing something in the room and ominously closes the double doors tight. Then he tiptoes across the room

Victor Oh, Haaaarlan! (*He stands in the middle of the room, listening*)

Harlan can be heard breathing heavily

(*Reacting to hearing the heavy breathing; moving around stealthily*) Do I hear a rat? A nasty smelly little rat? (*He suddenly turns and drives the axe into the bar*)

Harlan flies out from behind the bar and scampers for safety; he trips and sprawls

No need to call the exterminators. This one I can handle myself. (*He looms over Harlan with the axe raised*)

Colleen (*leaping out from her hiding place*) Victor! Don't do it!

Victor stops

Victor So, you're part of it too! Just as I thought! You told him about my plan, didn't you?

Colleen No!

Victor And I always thought you were so innocent! Well, you're lucky you're a woman, but for Harlan — (*looming over the fallen Harlan with the axe*) justice is going to be done! An eye for an eye, a head for a head!

Colleen I didn't tell him anything!

Harlan She didn't, Victor, she didn't! Listen to me — this is all a big mistake!

Victor You must have found this all so amusing! Stupid old Victor trying so hard to get himself killed! What a laugh! It must have been too much to resist! Well, I'm taking you with me, Harlan! You and I are both going to the great university in the sky! The land of eternal tenure! (*He raises the axe to strike the prostrate Harlan*)

Harlan Noooo!

Colleen rushes at Victor with a yell like a banshee and leaps on his back, flinging her arms around his neck and wrapping her legs around his waist. Harlan seizes the opportunity to get up and tries to grab the axe out of Victor's hands; both of them fight for possession. The three of them become a cluster of desperate wrestling bodies

Suddenly the double doors blow open and standing there out on the deck in the misty darkness, is a figure covered in a hideous half-decayed black shroud and holding a scythe

Victor AAAAGGHHH! What the hell's that?

Harlan's eyes go wide in terror. He lets go of the axe — leaving it in Victor's hands

Harlan Oh, my God! It's... It's ——

Colleen — it's the Grim Reaper! He's come ... He's come for Victor!

Victor *Oh, shit!* What does he want?

Harlan I think he's taking you to be judged!

The Grim Reaper points out into the night, as if to tell Victor to come with him

Victor Oh, no! (*Noticing the axe in his hand*) This really isn't a good time. (*Dropping the axe like a hot potato*) I know this all looks bad — but I've not been myself recently. I don't know what came over me just now! Trying to kill my friend here — (*dusting Harlan off, stroking his head*) it's completely out of character! It's just a phase I was going through, isn't it Harlan?

Harlan (*to the Grim Reaper*) Yes! Just a phase! You must be very familiar with all this, you know, the five stages of dying — denial, anger, bargaining for time, grieving, and then acceptance — happens to everyone ...

Colleen It's true! He's really a very nice guy!

Victor (*pleading*) I just need a little more time!

Harlan (*to the Grim Reaper*) You see — bargaining for time! (*Aside to Victor*) Tell him you have to talk to your loved ones!

Victor Yes! (*Beat*) Why?

Harlan You know — to get your life in order.

Victor Oh. Yeah, right. (*To the Grim Reaper*) Look, I'm not perfect, I'd be the first to admit it! But can't we hold off on this judging business for a while? Give me a chance to straighten a few things out before I go. I know I look like a heel right now, but I've learned my lesson! I'm a fast learner — straight "A"s all through school — and believe me, *I have got the message!* (*Pleadingly*) I'm just asking for a little more time! There's someone I have to talk to! I'm not ready yet!

There is a crash of thunder and the Grim Reaper points out into the darkness

(*Dropping to his knees in supplication*) No! Please — listen to me! *I'm not good with heat!* We're not talking about a couple of bad weeks in Tijuana, we're talking about eternity!

The Grim Reaper stands unmoved, hand still pointing into the darkness

Colleen (*to Victor*) Tell him why you became bad! It's your only chance!
Victor Yes! (*To the Grim Reaper*) Listen! I'm not saying I was right to have all those affairs! I've been bad! Bad! (*He slaps himself on the wrist*) It was wrong — I see that now! But there was a reason! I was betrayed!

Slowly the Grim Reaper puts down the outstretched hand and turns to Victor

Harlan He's going to listen! This is it, Victor — your big chance! (*He drags Victor in front of the Grim Reaper*) Tell him what happened!
Victor I can't! (*He runs away from the hideous apparition*)
Harlan (*grabbing Victor and pushing him forward*) You must! It's your only hope.
Victor It's no use! I'm doomed! I'm going to fry!
Harlan Victor, don't give up now! (*Slapping Victor*) Get a grip on yourself!

The slap has a sobering effect on Victor, but during the following speech he still hardly dares look at the Grim Reaper

Victor OK! Why did I go bad? Let me see — it all started three years ago. Dora — that's my wife — Dora said she was going to that art exhibit at the Backmann Gallery. She'd been acting strangely for a while — secretively — which is quite unlike her. I followed her. But she never went to the gallery that night. She went into a bar and met a man. I never saw his face, he always wore a hat and coat ... But she talked for hours — she met him more than once — always in dark out-of-the-way places where they wouldn't be recognized.
Harlan Three years ago?

Victor (*to Harlan*) Shhh! (*To the Grim Reaper*) Two years and eleven months to be exact.

Harlan starts to count on his fingers

That day is branded in my memory! I loved her and she betrayed me!

Harlan The *Pickwick* pub?

Victor Harlan, will you stop interrupt... (*Realizing*) Yes, the *Pickwick* pub! What about it?

Harlan And the *Latin Quarter Bar and Grill*?

Victor Yes!

Harlan Ah — that was me, Victor !

Victor You? *You!*

Harlan Yes. It was me. I was with Dora.

Colleen clutches her heart and faints again

Victor *You two-timing snake!* (*He grabs Harlan by the collar*)

Harlan Wait! Wait! It's not what you think! It was during the time that Helen was leaving me! I needed someone to talk to, that's all! I needed some advice!

Colleen revives, staggers to a chair and fans herself

Victor Advice? I don't believe you! Why would you go to Dora for advice? I was your best friend — why didn't you come to me? (*He tightens his grip on Harlan's throat*)

Harlan I couldn't! I felt so humiliated! I'm sorry, Victor, there are things that men can't talk to men about.

Victor There was no affair?

Harlan Of course not! Do I look like the kind of man Dora would have an affair with?

Victor You have a point. (*He loosens his grip on Harlan's throat then tightens again*) But what about that stupid hat and coat?

Harlan I didn't want the whole faculty and student body knowing Helen was leaving me. (*Sadly*) Not that it made any difference.

Victor (*letting go of Harlan's throat*) You should have come to me. I would have understood. (*Beat*) So you were my imaginary rival? (*He looks at Harlan and laughs*)

Harlan Yes. (*He laughs too*)

Soon they are both laughing hysterically at the ridiculousness of the situation

Victor You!

Harlan Yes! Me! (*Laughing*) And you thought ... !

They both convulse with laughter again. There is a sudden crash of thunder. Everybody jumps; they had quite forgotten about the Grim Reaper

Victor (*to the Grim Reaper*) Oh, please! Surely you've heard enough!

There is a flash of lightning and a roar of thunder. The sound of a strong wind rattles the cottage

Please — there must be something — you can't take me away now ...! (*He drops to his knees and crawls out on the deck to where the Grim Reaper is standing*) Not before I explain all this to my wife. (*He grovels at the Grim Reaper's feet*)

The wind blows stronger and the Grim Reaper points out into the darkness — pointing the way for Victor

Please! Have mercy on me! Have a little pity! (*He sobs and grabs the Grim Reaper's shroud, pulling on it while wailing for mercy*)

The shroud slips off and falls to the floor, revealing the Grim Reaper to be Dora

Dora Hello, Victor!
Victor (*staring at Dora*) What the hell! Dora?
Dora (*grinning at him*) Like my outfit? Just a few old things I found in the boathouse. An old boat cover, and I guess this — (*indicating the scythe*) is for clearing that damn brush. (*She comes into the room and puts down the scythe*)
Victor (*jumping to his feet*) *Jesus*, Dora!
Dora (*indignantly*) I can't believe you'd think I'd have an affair!
Victor What was I supposed to think? You never had any secrets from me before!
Dora Why didn't you confront me, you big dope? Why didn't you say something?
Victor Well, because — even a philosopher has some truths he can't bear to hear.
Colleen Does this mean that Victor's not dead?
Victor Yes! Now you've got me all confused! Am I alive, or is the real Grim Reaper going to show up any minute? (*He peers nervously into the darkness and closes the double doors tight*)
Dora There's something you ought to know about that gun. (*She goes to the bar, takes the pistol from its hiding place and aims it towards Victor*)

Victor Dora! What are you doing?
Dora The final revelation of the night, Victor!

Dora pulls the trigger. The pistol goes off with a loud blast. A red liquid oozes down the wall behind Victor

Victor feels himself all over thinking he has been shot. He hasn't. He looks behind him and sees the red liquid. Dora obviously aimed to miss him

Victor (*of the red stain*) What the hell ... ? What's going on?
Dora Just some cotton wadding soaked in red paint that I took from Colleen's paint box. I stuffed the wadding into your blanks, Victor.
Victor Paint? (*He goes to touch the stain with his finger*)
Dora Don't touch it!
Victor Huh?
Dora Not unless you want to keel over again. The paint is laced with "Sleeping Wolfsbane".
Victor What in God's name is "Sleeping Wolfsbane"?
Dora Just a little something I discovered in one of Colleen's books. It pays to keep an open mind about these things. The scientific name is "aconitinus somnifera". It grows like a weed around here. It's very powerful — even to the touch ... The Aleutian Indians smeared it on the tips of their harpoons to paralyze whales.
Victor Whales! Good God!

Suddenly the double doors are kicked open and Officer McGuire leaps into the room, pistol drawn

Officer McGuire *Freeze!*

Everybody almost leaps out of their skin — then they realize it is Officer McGuire

Harlan *I wish you wouldn't keep doing that, Officer!*
Officer McGuire (*aiming her gun at the others*) All right! What's going on? I was coming back from interviewing your neighbour when I heard another gunshot!

They all look at one another

Harlan A gunshot?
Officer McGuire Yes, a gunshot! And I heard it this time, so don't try any funny business! What the hell's going on in this cockamamie place? (*She looks at the upturned furniture, and sees the axe lying in the middle of the*

floor. She points her gun at it — she has the odd habit of aiming her gun at objects) Aha! And what's that doing there, eh? (*She sees the harpoon and aims her gun at it*) And that?

Harlan Oh, what's the use! Why don't we tell her the truth?

Officer McGuire That's more like it. (*She holsters her gun and flips out her notebook. She writes notes during the following*)

Dora All right. I did shoot Victor — at least I caused him to be shot. (*She indicates Victor*)

Victor points to the blood-stain on his shirt

Oh, I have to admit, that in a brief moment of madness I did think about using a real bullet ...

Victor You're kidding! I'd driven you to that?

Dora Yes, you had — but when I got down to Joe's Store and saw all those worms on sale, I had this awful vision of you lying in your grave and those horrible creatures eating you. It gave me a jolt of reality. You may have been a creep in recent years, but even you didn't deserve a fate like that. And we did have some wonderful times together before you went cuckoo on me. So, I just bought a large bottle of brandy and came home. But I was still mad. I couldn't concentrate on my studies. Then I remembered Colleen's stupid herbal books and I thought I could vent my anger on them — but instead I found the perfect solution. (*To Officer McGuire*) So I used some wadding laced with aconitine.

Officer McGuire With what?

Dora takes a small ball of red cotton wadding from her purse. The wadding is tightly bound with plastic kitchen wrap and tied off like a tiny sack. It is just big enough to fit into the barrel of the pistol, like the ammunition used in a paintball gun. Dora gives it to Officer McGuire who looks at the projectile like it's a dead rat

Dora Sleeping wolfsbane. It knocks you out.

Officer McGuire What are you talking about?

Colleen (*perkily*) You crush the root and squeeze it through a coffee filter. Quite easy really.

Dora gets the book "Herbs of The Northwest" from the shelf, and opens it to a bookmark

Dora Let me give you the official description. (*Reading*) "'Aconitinus somnifera'" also causes numbness of the tongue and mouth, and a sensation of ants crawling over the body —— "

Victor (*remembering*) Fire ants ...

Dora " — irregular and weak pulse, cold and clammy skin —— "

Victor Wait a minute! My pulse wasn't weak — it was gone! I checked with the stethoscope. (*He picks up the stethoscope*) I had no heartbeat!

Dora Oh, that! I stuffed the tubes with cotton wool.

Officer McGuire (*madly scribbling all this down*) ... had no heartbeat ...

Dora The other effects of aconitine are — (*reading*) "bloodless features, giddiness, staggering, physical collapse, but" — and this was the tricky part — "the mind usually remains clear." The Indian shamans use it in their ceremonies for soul-cleansing and enlightenment. I thought, hey, if it works for them it could work for Victor. (*To Victor*) So you see, we didn't know how much you could hear, so we had to play out this whole charade assuming that you could hear everything. It was very hard work.

Victor So my dream was just fragments of things I heard ... (*Something suddenly dawns on him*) What do you mean, we? (*He wheels on Harlan*) Were you in on this?

Harlan Me? Absolutely not. Dull Stoics don't get involved in childish pranks like that. (*He breaks into a grin*) Checkmate! Game, set, match! (*He does some funky jive body movements*) Slam dunk! Have I lost my touch? I don't think so! (*He offers Victor a high-five*) Gimme five, ol' buddy.

Victor You rat!

Officer McGuire (*scribbling in her notebook; trying to keep up*) ... staggering ... physical collapse ...

Dora (*to Victor*) I just wanted to give you a scare — the metaphysical stuff was Harlan's idea.

Harlan You see, after Dora calmed down, she told me what she'd seen and it didn't take us long to figure out that you weren't really having an affair with Colleen. At least, I was pretty certain.

Colleen (*indignantly*) Harlan!

Harlan No, I was really certain! At first I didn't want to get involved in the prank, but Dora convinced me that my life had turned into a passionless drift to oblivion. Get my butt off the sidelines and get back into the game, she said. And she was right. But most of all, we realized we had the perfect opportunity to shake you up — maybe even find out what was bothering you so much. We wanted to make this a learning experience for you, Victor. For all of us.

Officer McGuire (*still writing*) How do you spell "metaphysical"?

Victor All of us? You're not going to tell me Colleen was in on this too? (*To Colleen*) Please tell me there's a vestige of innocence left in this world. Please!

Colleen is silent for a moment, and then throws her arms in the air

Colleen Ta-dah!
Victor No!
Colleen It was for your own good, Victor. A kind of shock therapy, remember.
Victor The shock therapy was for *him*, not for me! Colleen, how could you do this? You're not the type!
Colleen (*gleefully*) That's what I thought, but you know, it was very exciting. I've never even held a gun before — (*to Officer McGuire*) and when you came bursting in with your gun drawn and everything — wow — I never thought we'd hold it all together — but we did! I've never felt so exhilarated in my life!
Harlan Hold it together! You shot the telephone right out from under my nose! That wasn't part of the plan! You scared the hell out of me, waving that gun around — a lump of wadding can still take your eye out!
Colleen Sorry, I got carried away in the excitement. You didn't give me a lot of time to prepare.
Harlan Well, never mind. (*Taking her in his arms*) You were magnificent, Colleen. You have joined the ranks of the great pranksters of history. (*He indicates the mask on the wall*) Puk-wudji would be proud.
Officer McGuire Who the hell's Puk-wudji?
Victor (*to Harlan, referring to Colleen*) I hope you realize you've created a monster. We'll never be safe again.
Harlan Cheer up! We've all learned something. I'd forgotten what fun life can be with a friend like you, Victor. It's been years since I felt so alive as I did tonight. We were right on the edge, pushing the envelope — my pulse was racing — my God, you even came at me with an axe! How long has it been since you've done that?
Officer McGuire (*writing furiously*) ... came at him with an axe ...
Victor I'm going to pay you back for this — big time!
Harlan Of course you are! I wouldn't expect anything less! But before you start planning the next prank, I suggest you ponder the lessons of this one. If my life with Colleen was a fraud, yours with Dora was a complete mess.
Victor You're right! Seeing my life flash before my eyes wasn't a pretty sight! (*Turning to Dora*) Dora, I know I've behaved mmm — badly, but I've never stopped — you know — and I was wondering if you — ah — still, ah ...

Beat

Dora Yes?
Victor I was wondering if you still ... Well, after all that's happened ... You know ...
Dora Yes?

Victor can't say it

Harlan Oh, for God's sake, Victor ! (*To Dora*) He wants to know if you still love him.

Dora Is that what you want to know?

Victor I need to know if we can start again — if there's enough love left ...?

Dora Of course I still love you! You think I'd go to all this trouble trying to have you shot if I didn't?

Victor Oh, this is wonderful! I'll make it up to you, Dora! (*He takes her in his arms and swirls her in a romantic dance*) We'll go on holiday — a second honeymoon! Anywhere you want to go! Just you and me! (*He sweeps Dora into a dramatic embrace right in front of Officer McGuire*)

Officer McGuire Before I throw up, let me remind you love-birds that the only place you're going is the slammer!

Dora On what charge, exactly?

Harlan Yes! It was all a game.

Officer McGuire Are you telling me that nobody's dead? Where's this Pukwudji guy?

Harlan (*indicating the mask*) There he is on the wall.

Officer McGuire wheels around and draws her gun — then sees it's just a mask

I'm sorry, Officer. Perhaps another time.

Officer McGuire holsters her gun and flicks frantically through her notebook

Officer McGuire There must be something ...! (*Desperately checking her notes*) Guns — axes — drugs — harpoons — bloodstains ... There's no way I'm not going to nail you on something.

Dora When you get there, let us know.

Officer McGuire You're saying this was all a prank?

Harlan Yes. That's what we've been trying to tell you.

Officer McGuire slowly tears all of the pages out of her notebook, scrunches them up and throws them away in disgust

Dora Will that be all, Officer?

Officer McGuire stares at them with annoyance. She tosses away the entire notebook. She starts to leave, stops and turns

Officer McGuire (*bursting with frustration*) You know something ...
Victor Yes?
Officer McGuire (*seething*) You people — deserve each other!

Officer McGuire turns to leave, trips on the axe still lying on the floor and goes flying. She angrily regains her composure and exits, slamming the door behind her

They all laugh. Victor embraces Dora; Harlan holds Colleen

Suddenly Officer McGuire kicks open the double doors

Officer McGuire (*shouting*) And clear that damn brush!

Officer McGuire exits

They all laugh

The Lights fade to black-out, apart from one small light illuminating the mask of Puk-Wudji the Trickster on the wall. The mask laughs, its previously solid wooden jaws moving hysterically; the sound of its laughter fills the theatre

Black-out

Music

CURTAIN

PRODUCTION NOTES

The Hidden Plot And The Visible Plot

The play is divided into two separate plots: the visible plot which the audience sees, and the hidden plot of which only some of the characters are aware. The hidden plot is revealed at the end of the play and should not become apparent to the audience until then.

In writing the play, I tried to adhere to the rule that every line should have a meaning that was ambiguous enough to service either plot. For example, in Act I, Scene 2, Dora says to Harlan, "You'll do it, then?" and he says, "Yes, I'll do it!" The audience should think they are both referring to Harlan agreeing to tell Colleen that he loves her (the visible plot), when the lines actually mean that Harlan has agreed to join Dora in the conspiracy against Victor and recruit Colleen into the conspiracy (the hidden plot).

To help the actors and the director, the following is an explanation of how and when the hidden plot unfolds. It is absolutely vital that this plot remains hidden and does not "bleed through" into the visible plot. The hidden plot should only appear clearly to the audience in retrospect with lots of small clues whose relevance was not obvious at the time.

The timeline is as follows. They have arrived for the weekend. It's a Friday. They left Vancouver early that morning and travelled up the coast using a combination of car ferries and roads, arriving at the cottage around noon with a stop at the village nearby for some supplies. Act I, Scene 1 starts in the early afternoon. They have done some unpacking and started vacationing. Victor has caught a fish, Colleen has been working on the mask she picked up in the village, and has gathered some herbs, etc.

The time lapse between Act I, Scenes 1 and 2 is quite a few hours. When Scene 2 begins it's evening, just around sunset, but it's summer and daylight lingers late in the day. The rest of the play is in real sequential time, so we see the sunset go to twilight and then to night. Since a lot takes place in the interval between the first two scenes, it is important that the audience feels some considerable time has passed. This can be done by showing that the exterior lighting has noticeably changed from bright daylight to late evening, plus the fact that the half-unpacked cardboard boxes and suitcases visible in Scene 1 have been put away.

What really happens between Act I, Scenes 1 and 2? At first Dora does consider putting real bullets in the gun, even going to the hunting supplies store. However, she calms down at the last minute and does not go through with buying the bullets.

Then Dora goes back to the cottage and talks to her confidant Harlan. They both realize that Victor is probably up to another one of his pranks and is not really having an affair with Colleen. Naturally, this is all unseen by the audience. Then Dora reads Colleen's herbal books where she gets the idea for the counter-prank against Victor to teach him a lesson.

Harlan is reluctant to get involved in Dora's counter-prank — despite its potential benefit to Victor — as he no longer believes in game-playing. However, his disastrous scene with Colleen makes him realize his stoicism is not serving him well and his relationships with both Victor and Colleen are suffering because of it. Dora's line, "It's time to get your butt off the sidelines and get back into the game", refers to the hidden plot against Victor.

Colleen participates because she believes that joining in a wild prank with her husband may free up his emotions in ways that will benefit their relationship, as well as to help Victor re-evaluate his nihilistic view of life and thereby reconcile with Dora.

Later, when Victor sees Harlan and Dora talking outside (after Dora's exit to go to the invented "Women's Guild Lecture"), Harlan and Dora are actually discussing the hidden plot. Victor almost figures this out when he says to Harlan: "Talking to Dora, were you? About me, I'll bet." Fortunately, Harlan manages to divert his thoughts away from this near-discovery of the hidden plot.

When Harlan does not shoot Victor the first time, the hidden plot gets unexpectedly derailed. Harlan was about to shoot Victor (following the plan), but Victor's sudden mention of Harlan's inability to "commit to Colleen", takes Harlan by surprise and he doesn't pull the trigger, so the opportunity is missed. After Harlan exits, Colleen (who has been observing the scene from outside) enters and tries to get the hidden plot back on track. She manages to do this by cleverly playing on Victor's dislike of being proved wrong in an argument, and predictably Victor can't resist another attempt to get Harlan to shoot him.

When Colleen exits through the double doors after Victor asks her to "Come back in five minutes", there is time for Colleen and Harlan to have a brief exchange about the plot outside before Harlan enters. This exchange is unseen by the audience, of course, and takes place while Victor looks around for the best location to put the pistol.

The rest of the hidden plot is a mixture of pre-planning and opportunism. The plot has moments where it spins out of control, like when Colleen gets too excited and overplays the scene over Victor's body — and when Victor goes on a rampage with the axe. At other times, it all unfolds perfectly according to plan, as in the scene with the blood-stained shirt and the stethoscope.

Use of the term "Indian"

The term "Indian" is used throughout the play, although this can be a sensitive issue in some areas. The more modern terms used in Canada are "First Nations", "Indigenous Peoples" or "Aboriginal Peoples", although the word "Indian" is still used in colloquial speech, especially by non-aboriginals. Well-educated individuals like the characters in this play are more likely to be early adopters of the current proper terminology. The situation also changes over time, which makes the use of any term in the published text problematic. "First Nations" is popular now, but despite its widespread use there is no legal definition for this term in Canada. It is not a synonym for "Aboriginal Peoples" because it doesn't include Inuit or Métis. "Aboriginal Peoples" is a collective name for all of the original peoples of Canada and their descendants. The Constitution Act of 1982 specifies that the "Aboriginal Peoples" in Canada consist of three groups — Indians, Inuit and Métis.

Whenever the play is performed outside Canada, the term "First Nations" may sound strange and confuse the audience. The United Nations uses the term "Indigenous Peoples". In the United States "American Indian" has been commonly used to describe the descendants of the original peoples of North America. Some people are dissatisfied with this term because it retains the misnomer "Indian" and covers peoples who consider themselves distinct from Indian peoples, namely the Inuit, Yupik and Aleut peoples in Alaska. A more approved term is "Native Americans". These terms are naturally not popular in Canada. In America the term "Indian" is still common among the tribes themselves as can be seen in their advertisements for "Indian Gaming".

All of these longer terms can be a mouthful when used in colloquial speech, so I have simply used the politically incorrect word "Indian". If you wish to substitute a more modern term, please feel free to do so as long as it sounds natural in the mouths of the characters. There is no doubt that the characters in the play would be familiar with the correct terms, although it would also be easy for them to slip back into old habits.

The gun

The script refers to a "point 44 Magnum, single-action revolver, five inch barrel, chrome finish, adjustable rear sights", but obviously use the technical description of the gun that you are able to get hold of. Try as hard as you can to get a silver or at least a light-coloured gun — it shows up much better on stage and catches the light in interesting ways. And make it as big as possible — it's the centerpiece of the suspense in the play. It must be a revolver not a semi-automatic, since almost everyone knows how to load a simple revolver. The bigger calibre also makes it more plausible that a piece of wadding large enough to deliver enough Wolfsbane to do the job would fit into the barrel.There is some debate over whether to say "point 44 magnum" or "44 magnum". I shall leave that up to the discretion of the speaker.

Pre-show and between-scenes music

The music should set a mood of foreboding and mystery. Since the play is set in the Pacific Northwest — the home of the Nootka, Haida and Kwakiutl — the music should reflect this heritage if possible. Music and the sounds of nature can add a lot of atmosphere to the play.

The following CDs have authentic Canadian First Nations music of the Pacific Northwest region on them:

Kwakiutl: Indian Music of the Pacific Northwest (1981): 2 CD set
Haida: Indian Music of the Pacific Northwest (1986): 2 CD set
Indian Music of the Pacific Northwest Coast (1967): 2 CD set

Look for these on www.worldmusicstore.com

If more dramatic music is required, any music that has an American Indian or Canadian First Nations influence can be used as long as it creates the right atmosphere such as the following:

Haida Way — from Shamanic Spirit by Alvin Kramer

Look for this on www.northstarmusic.co.uk

Harlan and Dora's relationship

In Act I, Scene 1 ("Why did I end up with a wild Epicurean philosophy professor, instead of a nice gentle Stoic like you?" etc.) it is important to show real warmth and friendship between Harlan and Dora. This sets up the revelation at the end of the play when Dora is the one Harlan turned to during the "Helen" crisis.

Changing the blanks

There are three different things going on here:

1. In the visible plot, Dora appears to take Victor's blanks out of the gun and replace them with what the audience thinks are real bullets. Her visible actions should make it look like she is inserting several bullets.

2. In the hidden plot she would actually be putting the wadding balls into the revolver's chambers and reinserting the blanks behind them as the propellant.

3. What is really happening on stage technically is nothing. It's all a mime show. None of the actual bullet-changing needs to take place as it is not seen by the audience since Dora's hands and the pistol are just below the level of the bar.

The Raven mask

Simple Mask

Transformation Mask

The mask of the trickster spirit Puk-wudji can be elaborate or simple depending on the resources of the theatre. The simplest one can be just a wooden mask with a fixed wicked smile. A little more complicated would be one with a wicked smile, but with wooden jaws that move when it laughs in the final scene. The most complex would be a true "transformation" mask in which the "smile" mask opens up to reveal another wildly laughing mask inside. Any of these will work, although the wood should look old and weathered. For those interested in Indian myths, Puk-wudji is an invented name although it is based on similar-sounding names. The rest of the description that Colleen gives about Raven is, however, real.

Raven is one of the most significant creatures in Northwest Indian art and mythology and is frequently seen in ceremonial masks. Among the Canadian First Nations he is usually referred to as just "Raven", rather than "The Raven". The mask of Raven has a long, usually straight, tapering beak, although the beak is also shown curved or squared at the tip. Raven is normally painted black with blue or green accents, and the nostrils, mouth and eyes are outlined in bright red and white paint. The "hair" is made from strips of cedar bark.

Raven plays many roles but mainly that of trickster, transformer and catalyst. He is a relentless schemer and practical joker, lustful, impulsive, and cunning. He loves to tease, cheat, woo and trick. With his magical powers, Raven can turn himself into anything at any time and can make almost anything happen by simply willing it to be so. Often, however, the tables would turn on the hapless Raven much in the same way as it happens to Victor in the play. While Victor starts out as the trickster, in the end he becomes the victim of his own trick.

Raven is often carved as a "transformation mask". A dancer wearing the mask swings his head from side to side as the mask is pulled open with strings, revealing the second mask inside.

N.B. The copyright in these designs is owned by the author; companies are free to use them without payment of any fee.

The harpoon

This is a simple Aleut harpoon, made of rough wood about five feet long with a bone point. Of course the point does not have to be bone, it can all be made of wood with the point painted white to simulate bone.

"Joe's Bait, Food & Ammo" grocery bag

This store is also a "Liquor Agency" as Dora buys some brandy there. For purists, the bag would also have the name "Liquor Agency" written on it somewhere. This is probably not necessary anywhere except in British Columbia where audience members may question how liquor was bought at a grocery store. In remote areas of BC it is common for grocery stores and gas stations to also act as liquor stores in an otherwise tightly regulated market.

Breaking the chess piece

The tension in Victor's hand over his being "wrong" snaps the chess piece in two. A chess piece can be made out of rigid Styrofoam (polystyrene) so that it breaks easily and gives a sharp snapping sound. It would have to be weighted to move like the other pieces.

The blood on Victor's shirt

The blood stain is in the area of Victor's heart, an area that is normally covered by his fisherman's vest. Colleen pulls the vest aside to reveal the blood when she rushes to his side after he has been shot. Victor only puts on the blood-stained shirt before the entrance that leads to him being shot — this entrance takes place just after Officer McGuire's first exit.

Shooting the telephone off the bar

There are three different things going on here:

1. In the visible plot, the audience thinks the phone base (an old black rotary works well) has been hit by a real bullet and knocked off the bar.

2. In the hidden plot, the phone base would be hit by a second backup piece of wadding put in the gun by Dora and knocked off the bar. In this scenario the phone would be splattered with the same toxic paint as the first shot, but since the phone base disappears behind the bar for the rest of the play this is not a problem.

3. What is *really* happening in the wonderful world of technical stage effects is that the phone base has been pulled off the bar by a stagehand pulling on a fishing line in time with the shot of a standard stage blank in the gun. The cord from the phone base to the receiver can be attached to the phone base with a piece of tape or Velcro, so that it simply pops off as the base falls. In past productions this has resulted in a very funny "dangling cord" effect, as if the power of the "bullet" has ripped off the cord too.

Dragging Victor's body offstage

The easiest way to achieve this is for Harlan to grab Victor's wrists and drag him along the floor. If you have a multi-level set with risers, this may be difficult, in which case Harlan has to pull Victor to an upright position and hoist him over his shoulder. Obviously this requires more practice. Another technique is to roll Victor on to a rug and drag the rug off stage.

When Dora comes back

Just after Victor's body is hidden, Dora returns. Dora is part of the plot, of course, but due to the sudden entrance of Officer McGuire, the conspirators don't have the time to talk to each other. Instead they are forced to gauge the situation with glances and body language since they are aware Victor may be able to hear their conversation and they also don't want to give the prank away to Officer McGuire. In Act II, when Dora is attempting to do a medical examination on Victor, she is genuinely trying to make sure that the dose of Wolfsbane is not too high to do him any real damage. Since he rejects all her offers and appears to be recovering from the effects of the Wolfsbane, she assumes that he is all right.

Dora's exit in Act II, leaving Victor with Harlan, is part of the pre-arranged plan for Harlan to convince Victor that he's a ghost.

Blood on the floor

When Officer McGuire sees the drops of blood on the floor, there does not actually have to be any blood visible. The smallness of the drops and the fact that the scene progresses very quickly means the audience readily accepts the fact that McGuire can see them.

Victor's dream

Victor's dream is actually the effects of Wolfsbane, where the body is in a state of physical collapse, but the mind is at least partly clear. These symptoms (as described in the final scene) are actually taken from the real description of Wolfsbane, but because Wolfsbane can be quite dangerous I created a fictional variant called "Sleeping Wolfsbane", implying that it is more benign than regular Wolfsbane in case there is a botanical expert in the audience. The part about the mind remaining clear when taking Wolfsbane is true, so Victor's dream is made up of fragments of dialogue that have gone on around him while he was semi-conscious.

The "whispering" scene

When Victor is outside on the deck looking for "Fish Facts Monthly", Harlan and Colleen have a scene where they discuss what to do with Victor. This is done for Victor's benefit, to set him up for the next scene where Harlan tells him he's dead. They actually want him to hear fragments of their dialogue, knowing that the more secretive they are, the more it will pique Victor's curiosity.

Harlan and the stethoscope

Harlan knows the tubes have been stuffed with cotton wool and therefore suggests that Victor use it. He uses the thermometer, which he knows will not work, as a roundabout way to lead Victor to the stethoscope. The thermometer's wooden backing makes it too big to fit in Victor's mouth.

Driving the axe into the stump

When the axe gets driven into the stump (or wooden table) on which the chess game sits, there is a balance between having an axe sharp enough to be embedded into the stump and safe enough for stage use. A layer of Styrofoam (polystyrene) or soft wood under the chess board would help as long as the chess board is securely fastened to the stump. Even if it does not stick to the stump, Harlan can hold the axe as if it is stuck until Victor throws the harpoon at him at which point Harlan can let go and drop it.

The Grim Reaper

When the Grim Reaper appears (s)he should stay as far outside in the misty night as possible and still be visible to the whole audience — the more shadowy and distant the figure, the more realistic (s)he will be. The costume is made up of an old mildewed tarp (a boat cover) and a scythe used for clearing the brush around the cottage. Whatever black material is used, it should be broken down to reflect something aged in a damp, cobwebby boathouse for many years. It's important that the arms and hands are well draped or gloved in black to disguise the fact that it is a woman's arms and hands.

The blood on the wall

When Dora "shoots" the pistol at the wall at the end of the play it is a regular stage blank. When the blood drips down the wall, this is easily done by having a few small holes in the wall through which a stage-hand squeezes a syringe or sponge filled with fake blood.

The cotton wadding

This is a small ball of cotton wadding, soaked with red paint. Since the wadding would be wet and toxic to the touch it is encapsulated in standard kitchen plastic wrap which would burst on contact rather like the projectile used in a paintball gun. The wadding is tightly bound with plastic wrap and tied off like a tiny sack. It is just .44 of an inch in diameter so it will look as if it will fit into the barrel of a good-sized pistol.

It is not actually used in the play, of course, only shown to Officer McGuire in the final scene.

THE CHESS GAME

(courtesy of Gregson Winkfield)

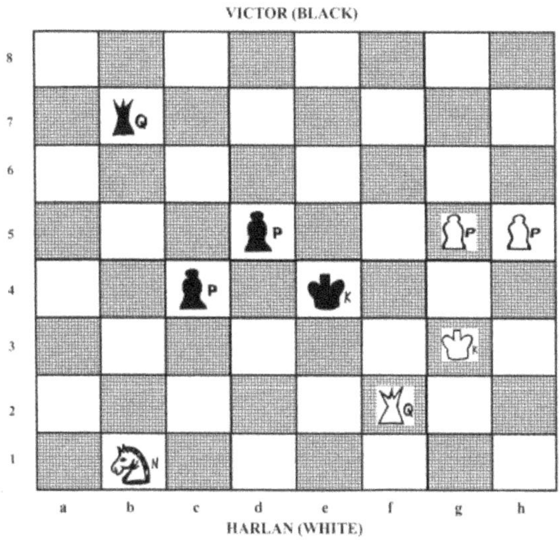

1. Victor's Black Queen takes White Knight on b1.
2. Harlan's White Queen goes to f4 - CHECK!
3. Victor's King moves to d3, forced.
4. Harlan's Queen moves to f5 - CHECK!
5. Victor's King moves anywhere legal.
6. Harlan's Queen takes Victor's Queen.

Peter Colley

FURNITURE AND PROPERTY LIST

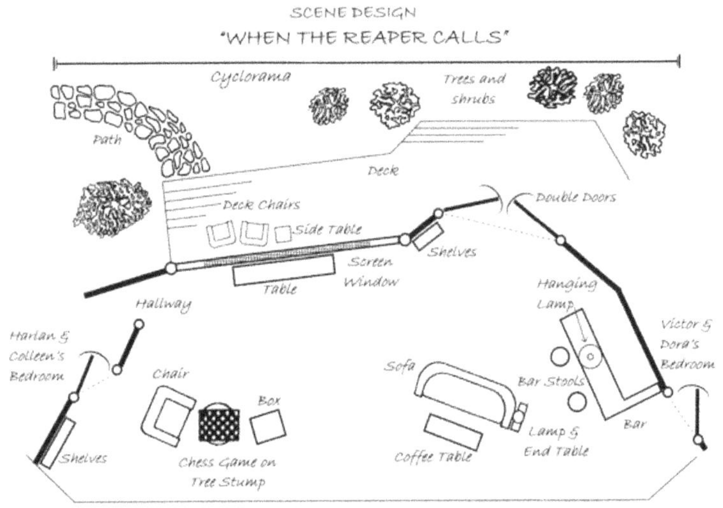

ACT I
Scene 1

On stage: Deckchairs
Beaten-up sofa
Small table made of tree stump or wooden crate. *On it*: chess set laid out as if in mid-game; one chess-piece is breakable (see Production Notes, p. 73)
Easy chair by chess table
Crate by chess table
Crude bar with bottles (including brandy); glasses; old telephone; newspapers, candle in short candlestick, matches. *By it*: bar stools, wastebasket. *Pinned nearby*: list of telephone numbers
Pile of firewood
Large woodchopper's axe
Half-unpacked cardboard boxes
Suitcases
Fly-swatter

Umbrellas
Bow with arrows
Aleutian Indian harpoon
Wall map of British Columbia coastline
Large wooden thermometer on wooden backing
On shelves: stacks of academic books including "Herbs of the Northwest"; freshly picked herbs in jam jars; diffusing pots; notepad and pen

Off stage: Fishing tackle box containing large silver-coloured revolver (**Victor**)
Partially-painted wooden Indian mask and box of paints (**Colleen**)
Doctor's bag containing stethoscope; big medical books (**Dora**)
Towel (**Dora**)
Tray of muffins (**Dora**)
Tray with cups of coffee on it (**Colleen**)
Philosophy book (**Harlan**)

Personal: **Victor**: watch (worn throughout)
Harlan: bifocal glasses (used throughout); watch (worn throughout)

Scene 2

Set: *In wastebasket*: plastic shopping bag with words "Joe's Bait, Food and Ammo" on it
On deck: "Fish Facts Monthly"magazine, fishing rod
Plato's *Apology* for **Harlan**

Strike: Half-unpacked cardboard boxes
Suitcases
Partially-painted wooden Indian mask and box of paints
Towel
Tray of muffins
Tray with cups of coffee on it

Off stage: Fully-painted wooden Indian mask (**Colleen**)
Fishing rod (**Officer McGuire**)

Personal: **Dora**: handbag containing red cotton wadding ball (see Technical Notes p. 73)
Officer McGuire: notebook

ACT II

Off stage: Scythe (Dora)

LIGHTING PLOT

Practical fittings required: pendant light over bar; lantern
One interior with exterior backing. The same throughout

ACT I, Scene 1

To open: General interior and exterior lighting. Summer sunlight

Cue 1	**Dora** laughs wickedly *Fade to black-out*	(Page 15)

ACT I, Scene 2

To open: General interior and exterior lighting with sunset effect. Pendant light on

Cue 2	As scene begins *Slowly fade exterior lights to twilight by p. 24 and then complete night with moonlight by p.27*	(Page 15)
Cue 3	**Victor** turns off the main room lights *Cut interior lights except pendant*	(Page 31)
Cue 4	**Victor** lights a candle *Bring up covering spot on candle*	(Page 31)
Cue 5	**Victor** pulls the cord to the pendant light *Snap off pendant light*	(Page 32)
Cue 6	**Colleen** enters with a lantern *Bring up covering spot on lantern*	(Page 32)
Cue 7	**Colleen** turns the lights back on *Bring up interior lights and pendant*	(Page 33)
Cue 8	**Colleen**: " … then I'll have to do it for you!" *Car headlights flash across the window*	(Page 35)
Cue 9	**Officer McGuire** exits into bedroom *Flash of lightning*	(Page 39)
Cue 10	**Victor**: "You all look like you've seen a ghost!" *Violent flash of lightning*	(Page 39)

Cue 11	**Colleen** faints again *Fade to black-out*	(Page 39)

ACT II

To open: Interior lights on as Cue 7; night with moonlight on exterior backing

Cue 12	**Harlan** helps **Colleen** up *Flicker of lightning*	(Page 40)
Cue 13	**Victor**: "Surely you've heard enough!" *Flash of lightning*	(Page 58)
Cue 14	**Officer McGuire** exits a second time. They all laugh *Fade to tight spot on mask*	(Page 64)
Cue 15	Mask laughs; when ready *Black-out*	(Page 64)

EFFECTS PLOT

ACT I

Cue 1	Before play begins *Music evocative of songs of Pacific Northwest Indians*	(Page 2)
Cue 2	When the play begins *Cross-fade pre-show music to sound of gentle wavelets and cry of a loon*	(Page 2)
Cue 3	**Victor**: "Don't ... don't ..." *Splash*	(Page 4)
Cue 4	**Dora** laughs wickedly; the lights fade *Ominous music; fade as Scene 2 begins*	(Page 15)
Cue 5	**Victor** exits into his bedroom L *Sound of door opening and closing off* R	(Page 16)
Cue 6	**Colleen** shoots *Base of telephone flies off bar (see Technical Notes, p. 70)*	(Page 35)
Cue 8	**Harlan**: "Someone must have heard the shots." *Rumble of thunder*	(Page 35)
Cue 9	**Dora**: "Hi, Colleen. Harlan." *Rumble of thunder*	(Page 36)
Cue 10	**Officer McGuire**: " ... Professor Pierce had gone?" *Louder rumble of thunder*	(Page 38)
Cue 11	Flash of lightning *Crack of thunder and double doors blow open. Mist effect around* **Victor** *outside double doors*	(Page 39)
Cue 12	Violent flash of lightning *Gust of wind rattles the cottage*	(Page 39)
Cue 13	The Lights fade *Music*	(Page 39)

ACT II

Cue 14	**Harlan** helps **Colleen** up *Rumble of thunder*	(Page 40)
Cue 15	**Victor** peers into the room. Pause *Sound of rustling leaves*	(Page 53)
Cue 16	**Colleen**, **Harlan** and **Victor** wrestle *Double doors blow open*	(Page 55)
Cue 17	**Victor**: "I'm not ready yet!" *Crash of thunder*	(Page 56)
Cue 18	**Harlan** and **Victor** convulse with laughter *Crash of thunder*	(Page 58)
Cue 19	**Victor**: "Surely you've heard enough!" *Roar of thunder. Strong wind rattles the cottage*	(Page 58)
Cue 20	**Victor** grovels at the **Grim Reaper**'s feet *Sound of wind increases*	(Page 58)
Cue 21	**Dora** shoots the pistol *Red liquid oozes down wall behind* **Victor** (*see Technical Notes p. 72*)	(Page 59)
Cue 22	Spotlight comes up on mask *Mask's jaws move hysterically; sound of loud laughter*	(Page 64)
Cue 23	Black-out *Music*	(Page 64)

MANAGEMENT OF FIREARMS AND OTHER WEAPONS IN PRODUCTIONS

Recommended reading:

Entertainment Information Sheet No. 20 (Health and Safety Executive).
This information sheet is one of a series produced in consultation with the Joint Advisory Committee for Broadcasting and the Performing Arts. It gives guidance on the management of weapons that are part of a production, including firearms, replicas and deactivated weapons.
It is obtainable from: HSE Books, PO Box 1999, Sudbury, Suffolk, CO10 2WA. Tel: 01787 881165, Fax: 01787 313995. Or it may be downloaded from: www.hse.gov.uk

Home Office Firearms Law: Guidance to the Police.
The Stationery Office 2002. ISBN 0 11 341273 8. Also available from: www.homeoffice.gov.uk

Health and Safety in Audio-visual Production: Your legal duties. Leaflet INDG360. HSE Books 2002

Lightning Source UK Ltd.
Milton Keynes UK
UKHW02f2135310518
323540UK00008B/244/P

9 780573 114779